JAKE BERNSTEIN

MARKET MASTERS

HOW SUCCESSFUL TRADERS THINK, TRADE AND INVEST*

*AND
HOW YOU
CAN TOO!

Dearborn
Financial Publishing, Inc.

While a great deal of care has been taken to provide accurate and current information, the ideas, suggestions, general principles and conclusions presented in this text are subject to local, state and federal laws and regulations, court cases and any revisions of same. The reader is thus urged to consult legal counsel regarding any points of law—this publication should not be used as a substitute for competent legal advice.

Publisher: Kathy A. Welton
Associate Editor: Karen A. Christensen
Editorial Assistant: Kristen G. Landreth
Interior Design and Typesetting: Professional Resources & Communications, Inc.
Cover Design: The Charles Marketing Group, Ltd.

Published by Dearborn Financial Publishing, Inc.

Printed in the United States of America

94 95 96 10 9 8 7 6 5 4 3 2 1

Library of Congress Cataloging-in-Publication Data

Bernstein, Jacob
    Market Masters : how successful traders think, trade and invest and how you can too! / Jake Bernstein.
      p. cm.
    Includes bibliographical references and index.
    ISBN 0-79310-587-0
    1. Floor traders (Finance)—United States. 2. Futures market—United States. 3. Stock-exchange—United States. I. Title.
HG4621.B475 1994   93-35779
332.64'5—dc20   CIP

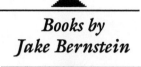

Books by
Jake Bernstein

Acknowledgments

Many thanks go to those who so willingly participated in my interviews. The time they gave me, albeit brief, will reap great dividends in assisting others on their path to wealth and success. Special thanks to Ellen Gordon, who assisted me greatly with all of the interviews. To my editor, Karen Christensen at Dearborn Financial Publishing, I owe a particular note of thanks for her patience and forbearance through the delays I encountered in finishing this book. Naturally, a word of thanks goes to my office staff who gave so kindly of their time through the numerous revisions and corrections. My family is owed a debt of gratitude for their tolerance during the manuscript process—a process with which they are well familiar but still takes its toll.

Finally, I wish to thank all of you out there, the readers who support the efforts of authors such as myself, for buying and finding something meaningful in my books.

Readers are welcome to write to me for assistance at the following address:

Jake Bernstein
MBH Commodity Advisors, Inc.
PO Box 353
Winnetka, IL 60093

Contents

Introduction

Without a doubt, the last bastion of capitalism is the futures market. Few areas in today's world of complex economics and investment strategies lend themselves as readily to potentially successful use by the average individual than do the futures markets. Yes, it is a known fact that most futures traders lose money. Yes, futures trading is perhaps among the most, if not *the* most, demanding of all undertakings in the area of speculation.

Yes, it is a known fact that those who speculate in such things as futures options have even less probability of success than do those who trade futures contracts. It is also true that the futures markets are extremely volatile and subject to substantial price moves within a matter of minutes. And, yes, professional traders have a distinct advantage over the average individual. Yet, given all the drawbacks, no other vehicle of which I am aware, offers as great a potential with, relatively speaking, such a limited amount of risk as do the futures markets. I do not mean to imply here that risk is limited. Certainly, the risk of loss in futures trading can be substantial. However, given the potential rewards, the risks are reasonable; given a method of well-defined risk management, futures trading is, to my way of thinking, the greatest game in town!

. . . given the potential rewards, the risks are reasonable; given a method of well-defined risk management, futures trading is, to my way of thinking, the greatest game in town!

Separating the Winners from the Losers

Vast fortunes can be amassed within a relatively brief period of time by trading futures. Naturally, the other side of the coin cannot be ignored. Vast fortunes may be lost in a relatively brief period of time in the futures markets. *What separates the winners from the losers in futures trading?*

This question has fascinated, intrigued, haunted, obsessed and frustrated traders since the first futures contract was traded hundreds of years ago. While one is tempted to take refuge in a plethora of intellectual and defensive responses, the answer to this question is indeed simple. Yet the simplicity of the response fails to do it justice inasmuch as the implementation of the response is, at least on the surface, exceptionally difficult. Scores of seminars, books, articles and lectures have attempted to cover the subject. But, as elusive as the keys to success may be, they are attainable through the use of various time-tested techniques.

The keys to successful trading are not only attainable; they can be learned and taught. *One of the most effective ways to learn is by example.* The interviews that follow in this book, along with the analyses of these interviews, will help illuminate the path to successful trading by way of example.

Lessons Learned from W. Clement Stone

On a hot Chicago summer day in the mid-1980s, I was fortunate enough to have an experience that changed my life as a trader. On a whim, several weeks earlier, I had called the offices of W. Clement Stone, the driving force behind Combined Insurance Company of America. Beginning with nothing more than determination and a vehemently positive attitude, Mr. Stone, or "Clem," built a vast insurance empire as well as a tremendous fortune. The Stone rags-to-riches story intrigued me. Given the close proximity of Mr. Stone and his empire to my home, I asked if I could interview him. To my surprise, he agreed.

With several "attendants" at his side, Clem arrived at his corporate studios, perfectly dressed—suit, white shirt and ascot, his imposing mustache curled and tailored perfectly. When Clem entered the room, I felt a certain respect that, to this day, I cannot describe. The man exuded self-confidence; he made every movement with self-assurance and singleness of purpose. He reached out his hand, and I took it. His handshake was solid, purposive and firm. He looked me straight in the eye—a piercing, deep and all-knowing look.

Attitudes Versus Luck

I told Stone that I was indeed privileged to interview him, and I stated my purpose for the meeting, which was to gain some insight into his business philosophy and moreover his psychological techniques for maintaining a positive mental attitude throughout the years. The question on my mind was whether Stone's attitudes were truly major forces underlying his success or whether he just happened to be in the right place at the right time. This question is always asked of those who are successful, but it can be answered only after an examination of the pertinent facts. Some traders claim success is based on having a "lucky break." Others claim that success is based on knowing the right people. Still more claim that success is based on positioning. I do not agree, nor would W. Clement Stone.

Positive Mental Attitude

In addition to Stone's vast wealth and business empire, he is most recognized for his preaching of *positive mental attitude* (PMA). Along with such notables as Og Mandino, Norman Vincent Peale and Napoleon Hill, Stone claims that the power to achieve comes from within and that positive motivation overcomes all obstacles to success. Those who maintain the PMA point of view argue that to be at the right place at the right time, one must have the correct attitude to recognize the opportunity for success.

The PMA group has given the world numerous books, tapes and publications—all designed to educate the U.S. on the benefits and techniques of positive mental attitude. While I believe that PMA is truly valuable and that it should be studied by all who are interested in achieving and maintaining success, many feel otherwise. Positive attitudes cannot be replaced by such vague and fleeting concepts as luck, positioning or political influence. I do not claim that other methods of achieving success are not effective; rather, to facilitate the functioning of these other techniques, one must first have a solid base of positive mental attitude. The individual who seeks to succeed by creating opportunities through political manipulation must be confident in his or her abilities, or success will not come.

Whether we agree that positive mental attitude facilitates and enhances success, the fact remains that in the struggle for success in futures trading, a negative attitude easily spells ruin, just as the lack of a positive attitude easily inhibits success. Recognizing this fact, I found what follows in my interview with W. Clement Stone not only exceptionally interesting from an academic point of view but extremely powerful and helpful in my futures trading.

▲
_____

... in the struggle for success in futures trading, a negative attitude easily spells ruin just as the lack of a positive attitude easily inhibits success.

_____
▼

I asked the pertinent question: "Mr. Stone, you are among one of the most successful individuals in American history. What contributed most to your success?" What follows is a very close approximation of his response.

Think, See and Do

"To be successful, you need to cultivate and practice three important elements. When I was 7 years old, I had my own newspaper route. When I was 11, I had my own newspaper stand. When I was 16, I began to sell insurance. I went to the bank building in town and approached the desk of the bank president. I said, 'Sir, may I take a moment of your time?' He looked at me and said, 'Son, are you here to sell me something?' I answered, 'Yes.' He said, 'Then don't ask for a minute of my time. *Take it!*' " At this point, Stone looked me straight in the eye as if to say that he had made a significant point. I replied with a look of acquiescence to indicate that I understood exactly what he meant.

Stone continued, "To be successful, you need to incorporate three elements into your plan. First, you must *think*. You must think about what you want to do and how you will do it. Next, you must *see* an opportunity as it develops. And last, you must *act* when the opportunity presents itself. You must think, see and do. Those are the important elements to success." These important words unlocked a new and effective strategy for my career as a futures trader. I realized that I had not achieved even a small fraction of my potential as a trader since I had approached my market work haphazardly and without a predisposition to success.

▲

"You must think, see and do. Those are the important elements to success."
W. Clement Stone

▼

To begin with, I wasn't really thinking; rather, I was hoping. I hoped for success and in vague terms; I organized for it. However, when it came to visualizing a plan of attack, I was sorely lacking. Secondly, I did not visualize opportunities when they presented themselves. Because I was so intent on not missing opportunities and unsure about what opportunities I was looking for, I failed to see them when they presented themselves. And, failing to see opportunities, I could not act in a fashion that yielded successful results. In other words, I was sorely lacking in all three of Stone's elements to success. Knowing this, I altered significantly my behavior and opened the doors that eventually lead me to success as a trader. Without Stone's words on that fateful day, my path to success would have been difficult, if not impossible to follow.

What This Book Can Do for You

I do not claim to be as motivational a speaker or writer as W. Clement Stone or his PMA colleagues. Nor do I promise that this book will change your life as a trader. However, I can make you some promises about the value of this book:

◆ Studying the interviews and, in particular, the analysis of the interviews in this book will give you important insights into the thought and action processes of individuals who, through their efforts and motivation, have become respected figures in the field of stock and commodity trading.

◆ Comparing your behaviors and attitudes with those of accomplished market analysts and traders will either confirm or negate your orientation and may therefore alert you to changes you may want to incorporate into your behavior and trading.

◆ Reading this book will give you important tools to assist the developmental process that tends to typify those who have been successful in the markets.

A Book for Individuals

As you read *Market Masters*, make comparisons to your own situation and seek out behaviors, attitudes and methodologies that appear to fit your needs and personality. In so doing, remember above all that *what you do in the markets must fit your temperament*. The stock and futures markets offer many opportunities. Vastly different styles of trading may yield success, but not every avenue is suitable for every individual. Just as life itself offers a multiplicity of different expressive avenues, so do the stock and futures markets. While one individual may be well-suited for the demanding position of a floor broker, another person is at ease trading long-term positions and infrequently checking the prices. Either avenue may lead to wealth. Then again, neither avenue may lead to wealth if the skills necessary for success have not been mastered. Remember, above all else, that this book is not a Holy-Grail, perfect-trading-system, get-rich-quick, never-lose, isn't-futures-trading-great book.

Market Masters is for individuals who are individuals. It is for those who do not wish to follow the crowd but who wish to follow the lead of a few successful individuals who have achieved success through hard work, persistence and consistency.

Think, see and do—wealth will follow. Although many contemporary books on personal growth and psychology stress the importance of keeping your eye on the goal, I feel that keeping your eye on the concept and acting on opportunities are more important. Jesse Livermore, legendary speculator of the early 1900s, said, "Profits take care of themselves; losses tend to get worse." And so it is with one's personal orientation to the markets.

Success Follows

Success tends to take care of itself if you provide the proper psychological and behavioral backdrop for it to occur. Goals are indeed wonderful; without them, we would all proceed haphazardly about our lives, randomly finding success and possibly not even recognizing it once it has come our way. Yet, the road to success must be paved with behaviors, attitudes, opinions and visualizations.

Theoretical Framework

My theory on and orientation to the issue of trader success is based upon four elements. These elements form the underlying structure of what I will attempt to demonstrate through the interviews that follow. I am not presenting a psychological evaluation or clinical examination of the responses to my interview questions. As you will see, each individual has his own brand of personal psychology. The individual's personal psychology does not interest me, nor do the methodological considerations that were used to achieve success. Instead, each individual's response style intrigues me because it reveals a great deal about how a person who has been successful approaches the markets and, above all, copes with the many reversals that are, unfortunately but necessarily, such a significant part of futures trading.

Here then are the four elements that comprise the essence of my success theory:

1. The way in which traders deal with loss and failure is just as important, if not more important, than the way in which they deal with success.

2. Effectively controlling and channelling emotions are two primary issues in the equation for success.

3. Those who have been successful and continue to be successful either as traders or as market analysts, trading advisers or market experts recognize the importance of market psychology and, to a certain extent, incorporate it into their work.

4. There are core elements common to the behavior of successful market professionals; to be successful in the markets, you need to develop and maintain similar attitudes, behaviors and opinions.

From Reality Back to Theory

Remember, my theoretical framework does not seek to pigeonhole all traders into a given response style or set of attitudes. Rather, it works from reality back to theory. Let me clarify what I mean. Some explanations of phenomena begin with a theory or hypothetical construct. They begin with a set of assumptions based on logical alternatives, which in turn are based on known scientific, psychological or sociological facts. These theories then work forward amassing a body of evidence to either confirm or negate their validity.

My approach is distinctly different. While I begin with a theoretical exposition on the subject of trader success, this conclusion has been derived from a pragmatic or empirical orientation. I did not wake up one day and decide that my theory of market success must be based upon trader psychology. Rather, I studied successful traders and analysts and extracted common elements in their behaviors, which thereby allowed me to construct a theory or explanation with the advantage of factual support.

The information in this book should not be taken as supportive of a scientific or quasi-scientific theory of trader behavior. In fact, much of the information is anecdotal and unsupported by hard evidence other than the experiences, results and considered opinions of those who have the credentials of success to justify the value of listening to their ideas and learning from their experiences.

Understanding Failure

It has been said that we learn more from our mistakes than we do from our successes. Although success is important, understanding failure and its role in shaping trader behavior is equally important. E.L. Thorndike, the father of American Psychological Learning Theory, observed so insightfully that millions of behaviors are wrong, but only a handful of behaviors are right. By punishing for trading errors, either our own or those of others, we are not really learning anything. Because traders may do many wrong things and so few right things, to punish for those wrong things would simply open the door for something else that is wrong. The idea is not to punish or ridicule that which was done wrong but rather to understand it, correct it and to do it right so that the rewards of being right may solidify the winning behavior.

The Weak Link

The markets offer fortunes without limit to those who master the few simple rules of profitable trading. As I stated before, the rules are simple but their implementation is difficult because human beings ultimately are the ones who must implement trading decisions and market timing signals. The weakest link in the chain is, has been and always will be the trader. *Do not fall victim* to the same perception that has proven to be the downfall of so many traders before you and that most assuredly will prove to be the undoing of many traders after you. *Do not fall victim to the belief that a better trading system will make you a better trader.* The most sophisticated and potentially successful trading system in the world will prove to be nothing more than a tool of self-destruction.

The weakest link in the chain is, has been and always will be the trader.

The world's best trading system in the hands of an incompetent, undisciplined and unsophisticated trader will prove to be the vehicle for consistent losses. I do not imply that a good trading system cannot help you succeed. Indeed it can! Yet, no matter how good your trading system may be, you are the only one who makes that system work as it was intended unless, of course, you hire an experienced and disciplined professional.

Consider a trading system that is so profitable it generates, within a short time, thousands of dollars. Then, consider a period of *drawdown*, which is a necessary part of all trading systems. The drawdown is really what makes or breaks a trading system. If the individual who is trading the system limits drawdown to what it should be, based on the trading signals generated by the system, then the system will recoup and move on to bigger and better things. However, if the individual is undisciplined, unwilling to accept losses when they should be taken according to the system, the drawdown period will either be longer than intended and/or the dollar amount of drawdown will be greater than intended or greater than it should have been. The system will deteriorate because of the trader.

I maintain that the ability of a trader to cope with such periods of drawdown and losses will either make or break a system. No matter how good a system may be, this, the weakest link in the chain, will break the back of the system and the trader more quickly than any unexpected event. At this point, the psychology of the trader becomes of paramount importance; attitudes, behavior, perceptions and experience become the quintessential elements for success.

By correctly applying what has been learned through experience, and by coping with losses, the trader will either make or break the system. While no predetermined formula exists for dealing with such situations, there are methods and procedures that may either minimize the degree of trader error or maximize it depending upon the trader's response style.

Shortcut to Learning

You can learn the elements to successful trading in different ways. For example, you can undergo a lengthy period of psychiatric treatment that may or may not be of value. You might enroll in a success motivation course that will likely help you succeed. You can read extensively about futures trading and investing in the stock market to develop your own methods and procedures. You may read the writings of master traders and speculators to extract the most meaningful methods and procedures. You might embark on a course of finding the perfect trading system only to discover that it will not help you. Or you can shortcut all the above by going directly to Jack Schwager's *Market Wizards* books or to the information provided in this book.

Either way, your goal should be to focus upon technique and trader psychology as opposed to market methodology or trading systems. I estimate that a trading system is only 20 percent of the necessary ingredients for success in the stock and/or futures markets. The balance consists of effective risk management tools, positive mental attitude, personal trader psychology, discipline, structure, consistency and persistence. All these can be learned, but, like anything else that is worthwhile, practice, patience and persistence are the critical tools in successfully bringing you to your goal.

. . . your goal should be to focus upon technique and trader psychology as opposed to market methodology or trading systems.

Visualize, Recognize and Act

I hope that the interviews and analyses that follow help you on your road to success as a trader. Remember, however, that to win the battle as opposed to winning only brief battles, you need to think, see and do. *You need to visualize opportunities, recognize them when they appear and, above all, consistently act on them once they present themselves.* You need to act without concern as to whether these opportunities will produce profits or losses because the success of any trading signal or any investment can be known only partially prior to its actual occurrence. Do not fall into the trap of thinking that the trade or investment you are about to make will not be successful. It has no greater or lesser chance of success than does any other signal derived from your system.

Winning Attitudes and Behaviors

Every signal generated by your trading system or method of market analysis must be considered at the outset to be the signal that will produce a vast fortune. If you do not look upon each trading opportunity as a significant opportunity for profit, you will allow yourself to be dissuaded from acting accordingly. If you do not enter each trade with a positive attitude, you open the door to self-doubt, which is among the greatest enemies that defeats a trader.

No individual, no course, no tape, no lecture, no article, no book can do for you what you can do for yourself. To develop winning attitudes and behaviors, you need to work with yourself, and you need to develop your skills through your own efforts. In so doing, you have only a limited amount of time, and you must therefore be selective about what you seek to study. My advice, which is based on considerable experience, is to focus on your personal growth as a trader by studying the elements that have made others successful in this field.

The
Market Masters

Sed omnia praeclara tam difficilia quam rara sunt . . . "But everything great is just as difficult to realize as it is rare to find . . ." are the closing words of philosopher Spinoza's great work, *Ethics*.

Whether greatness is achieved in art, science, business or philosophy, it is rarely an overnight phenomenon. Some of the most accomplished individuals, often considered "overnight successes" in their field, realized their greatness only after years of effort and thousands of failures. What seems obvious and apparent on the outside often bears little resemblance to what is inside. It seems somewhat blasphemous to borrow from one of history's greatest thinkers to make a point about success as a stock or futures trader. However, if my application of Spinoza's wisdom helps you achieve greatness as a trader or as an investor, then applying his teachings to trading psychology will be worthwhile.

Years of Experience

Frequently, I am asked what I have learned in more than 22 years as a stock and futures trader. At times, I respond that what I have learned could easily fill 20 books; yet I realize that I have learned little. However, the value and intensity of what I have gleaned from my years of experience are significant. As in the case of anyone who attempts to be successful as a trader, I found it difficult to realize my success both in terms of the actual process and in terms of recognizing my own success.

The road to profits is lined with the best intentions, the best trading systems and the most disciplined trading plans. Consistent success is not only difficult to realize but hard to find. It is the rarest of all commodities.

Through the years, I have shared with other traders the knowledge I have accumulated through my long and often hard experiences. In my book, *The Investor's Quotient* (1980), I set forth the principles that govern investor and trader behavior. I provided numerous suggestions as to how losing behaviors might be transformed into positive behaviors and attitudes. In *Beyond the Investor's Quotient* (1988), I expanded on the techniques and insights offered in *The Investor's Quotient*. In 1993, I wrote *The New Investor's Quotient*, which updated the concepts and techniques provided in the original edition and expanded on new methods that had developed since 1980.

Yet in spite of everything I have written and spoken about regarding trader behavior since 1972, the trader's lot has not improved significantly. Traders, for the most part, are still victims of myriad weaknesses and shortcomings, demons of their own creation. Most limitations can be corrected easily, but none can be changed without varying degrees of effort.

The Ostrich Syndrome

Modern techniques of psychological and behavioral treatment are numerous and effective. Today, no trader should continue on the same path of blunders that has inhibited success for so many years. But the trader is human. Given the frailties of the human ego, it is difficult for the trader who realizes that psychological difficulties are inhibiting his or her success to seek professional assistance in remedying these problems. Most traders, believing erroneously that a "better trading system," a "faster computer," or "more historical research" will be the panacea to what has inhibited their success, continue to struggle with themselves and with the market. Many traders refuse assistance because they have been told that they can "do it themselves." They do not admit weakness. They do not let others know that they have lost control over their emotions or that they had little control in the first place.

I have labored long to find a solution to this *ostrich syndrome* that afflicts so many traders. I realize that the same methods and techniques will not be sufficient for all traders. While a great deal can be said for books, tapes, seminars, group therapy and one-on-one therapy, these methods do not guarantee success no matter how strongly their proponents extol the virtues of their methods.

How You Can Benefit from Trader Psychology

After many years as a trader and an observer of trader behavior in the futures markets, I am convinced that a trader must know which behaviors must be changed to achieve consistent success. A trader must also know which new behaviors must be learned to replace dysfunctional or negative behaviors.

Knowledge from the Experts

While I could easily bend your ear with lists of suggestions and observations, I think that the better approach is to share with you the knowledge I have acquired through the analysis of a series of interviews with individuals who are respected for their achievements in the stock and futures industries. In futures trading, as in most endeavors, nothing succeeds like success. The key is to isolate what constitutes success and to learn from the triumphs of others as well as from one's own achievements.

▲

The key is to isolate what constitutes success and to learn from the triumphs of others as well as from one's own achievements.

▼

The Trader's Worst Enemy

The idea for this book originated many years ago but was not developed until recently because of my belief that traders would eventually find their own way and improve their ability to profit consistently from the markets. Time has proven me wrong. Time has shown me that *for one reason or another, traders and investors continue to trip on their own emotions and fail as a result of their own shortcomings.* Sad but true, the trader's worst enemy is, has always been and probably always will be his or her own self. I have observed hundreds, perhaps thousands, of occasions when traders have taken effective trading systems, outstanding recommendations, highly successful advice and otherwise solid analytical information, and used them not only ineffectively but to distinct disadvantage. If this had occurred infrequently or accidentally, I could write off my observations to chance. However, the pervasiveness and repetitiveness of such behavior in virtually every individual at one time or another has lead me to conclude that as an experienced trader I must try to rectify the situation or at the very least improve it.

▲

. . . traders and investors continue to trip on their own emotions and fail as a result of their own shortcomings.

▼

A New Focus

Before writing this book, I focused on recognizing, analyzing, eliminating and replacing behaviors that limit performance in the market. Though I have received many letters and telephone calls through the years praising my efforts and thanking me for results achieved due to my information, it is still not enough.

At this juncture, the best approach is a positive one that focuses on recognizing and accentuating behaviors that have facilitated the success of others. Why not study successful market analysts and traders to determine precisely what they have done, either externally through behavior or internally through thought processes or attitudes, to succeed at speculation and investing, two of the most difficult undertakings that traders and investors can attempt?

The Interviews

Who should I interview? I avoided interviewing market professionals who have already been featured in books such as Jack Schwager's *Market Wizards*. Rather, I searched for individuals whose experiences, understandings and insights can be used effectively by futures and stock traders inasmuch as their perspectives are somewhat different, given their varied positions in the futures industry. Furthermore, I chose individuals who I have known personally either as colleagues or as business associates.

George Angell

George Angell is highly skilled in *technical analysis*. His extensive experience as a floor trader, day trader and spread trader offers valuable insights to newcomers and seasoned traders alike. George's personal experiences during his years of trading can serve all of us well.

Gerald Appel

Gerald Appel is known as the *father of moving average convergence divergence* (MACD), an indicator he developed for the purpose of trading stock index futures. He is an accomplished professional trader who has achieved both the respect and recognition of his peers as a highly disciplined and innovative trader. He brings to *Market Masters* his skill, insights and observations.

Bruce Babcock

As "watchdog" of the futures advisory industry, Bruce has seen all too many traders, systems, advisers and hotlines come and go. Bruce is an active trader and devoted researcher. As long as I have known Bruce (at least ten years now), he has been direct, analytical and deeply dedicated to his work as well as his trading. His observations and insights are offered herein with the hope that you will find them as valuable as I have.

George Lane

George is the *father of stochastics*. He is indeed the foremost authority on stochastics and a keen observer of futures trading and futures traders. I have known and respected

George for more than 20 years. Few individuals can match his level of expertise or, for that matter, his iconoclastic, "shoot from the hip" style. He is indeed the *granddaddy* of futures trading with much to offer.

Conrad Leslie

Conrad Leslie and I go back many years as players in the same difficult game. Yet Conrad has experienced much more than I have in terms of *fundamental* research. His role as an authority on crop forecasting has not prevented him from growing both philosophically as well as technically. Conrad can teach us a great deal—all we need do is to listen and act accordingly.

Robert Prechter

I interviewed Robert Prechter of the *Elliott Wave Theorist*, a man I have known for many years and one for whom I have great respect as an individual doggedly dedicated to his analytical methodology. For years, I have felt that Bob's knowledge of trader psychology is perhaps equal to, if not greater than, his vast achievements as a market technician. I had been convinced that the Elliott Wave, Bob's lifework, is primarily an emotionally inspired pattern, and his interview confirmed my belief. My questions to Bob therefore focused precisely on his understandings of market psychology with only passing mention of his preeminence as an Elliott Wave analyst.

Welles Wilder

Welles Wilder is known throughout the world for his development of numerous trading methods, as well as the *relative strength indicator* (RSI), which has become synonymous with Wilder's name. In the early 1980s, Welles and I, along with a group of other traders and analysts, toured the Far East presenting a series of futures trading seminars. I recognized Welles's true talent as a trader, and I admired his ability to remain detached, calculatedly analytical and exceptionally realistic about the markets.

Larry Williams

Larry Williams has found himself in the midst of numerous controversies through the years, many of which have centered around his aggressive promotion of trading systems and seminars. Quite candidly, as Larry will be the first to admit, he is a hero to many and a villain to others. I will always remember Larry's aplomb and confidence as he methodically parlayed $10,000 to well over $2 million in the Robbins World Cup of Futures Trading Championship, only then to give back about $1 million before the contest ended.

Larry has been a great contributor to futures and stock trading not only in terms of techniques and methodologies but as *an individual whose approach to futures trading must serve as a model to all traders aspiring to succeed.*

The Elements of Success

I am fortunate, indeed gratified, that these individuals agreed to be part of *Market Masters*. I know that their contributions will be appreciated by every reader.

My hope is that the analyses that follow each interview, as well as the overall analysis of the interviews collectively, will help pinpoint specific areas of commonality among the experts interviewed so that you can extract and eventually develop within yourself the personal skills that have facilitated the success of these well-known individuals. You will note that the people interviewed for this book have distinctly different backgrounds and substantially diverse points of view about most matters, yet they share in common elements that I feel are inherent to successful traders and analysts.

Offered herein are the quintessential elements of success as a trader or as an investor, and I urge you to explore, understand and integrate them into your trading approach so that they may facilitate and enhance your success as they have done for so many other traders and investors.

Methodology, Assumptions and Techniques

My interview techniques were simple. To obtain the greatest amount of useful information from each individual, my questions were as general and open-ended as possible. In some instances questions related to the individual's methods or achievements and therefore were more specific. The general list of questions were as follows:

- ◆ What precipitated your desire to trade, and when?
- ◆ What qualities do you feel contributed most to your success as a trader?
- ◆ Do you use specific techniques for coping with losses?
- ◆ Estimate what percentage of a trader's success is a direct result of a good system as opposed to trading skills. What would be the split?
- ◆ What is the greatest lesson you learned in your life as a trader?
- ◆ Do you feel your success was inspired by any famous traders? If so, who, and how so?
- ◆ Are you in touch with any specific experiences that either facilitated or inhibited your trading success?
- ◆ Do you have any favorite techniques for emotionally dealing with periods of drawdown?
- ◆ What advice would you give to new traders interested in using some of your techniques?

Some questions were altered to accommodate specific interests of the individuals being interviewed; however, for the most part, this is the core of questions presented. A complete list of questions is included with each interview.

My Goals

My goals in each interview were as follows:

◆ To extract as much information as possible on the subjects covered.

◆ To obtain answers that were as specific as possible in relation to each question.

◆ To engage each expert in a thought process that would yield responses meaningful to my readers.

◆ To provide responses that would lend themselves to an overall analysis to ascertain any common elements or lack thereof among our different experts.

Assumptions

Although I entered into the interviews with certain basic assumptions regarding what I might find, I allowed for the option of changing them if I should discover that my original assumptions were incorrect. Some of my more significant assumptions follow:

◆ Common elements among the experts would exist not only in the areas of emotional response to the markets but in areas of discipline and experience as well.

◆ The experts would agree generally as to the importance of psychological issues in forming successful trader behavior.

◆ Most experts would attribute their success to the same basic qualities.

◆ The experts would share similar learning experiences in the markets that helped shape their successes.

Format

To evaluate the interviews objectively, each interview chapter has the following format:

◆ An entire chapter is devoted to each interview.

◆ Each chapter begins with a brief biography of the individual, as given to us during the interview.

◆ Each response is evaluated in terms of common elements in the following general areas.

Similarity of experiences. Were any experiences important in shaping attitudes, behaviors and expectations? If so, how were they similar? If not, how were they different? What can be concluded about the experiences that shape winning behaviors?

Similarities and/or differences in attitudes and opinions. How do the attitudes and opinions of each individual compare to one another? Are there common elements?

Methods of dealing with emotion. What methods does the individual use in dealing with emotional responses to various market conditions and events? How are these similar to or different from those of other experts interviewed?

Recommendations to other traders. What general recommendations are given to other traders by our experts to help them achieve and maintain trading success?

Importance of a trading system. How important does the expert feel a trading system is in the overall attainment of success as a trader?

Evaluation

After the presentation and discussion of the interviews, you will find an evaluation of the important common elements and differences to determine what can be learned from the experts' experiences. You will also find specific suggestions in every major area of investor and trader behavior.

The Chosen Few

You may wonder why I interviewed market analysts and traders as opposed to interviewing only traders. My goal in writing this book is to assess particular behaviors and attitudes within a concise theoretical framework. The individuals selected are, in many cases, public figures and therefore easily identified with. Given my many years of training and experience as a psychologist, I felt that my method of analysis would be quite meaningful to traders on a personal level.

My reasons for selecting these individuals are as follows:

◆ They are known by traders throughout the world and have achieved a significant public following of their work during the years.

◆ Given their lengthy experience, both in market methodology and as traders, these individuals are in a better position to identify with the "average" trader than are those who strictly trade or manage money. They have had significant contact with the trading public and are familiar with the problems that face most traders today.

◆ They have experienced many different types of market environments through the years and by virtue of their longevity are capable of expressing meaningful opinions derived from their vast experiences.

◆ It is important to understand the psychology of those who have had more ups and downs, more trials and tribulations than have money managers who became overnight successes or who were not subjected to as much adversity.

Open to Change

To truly master trading, an individual must be open to evaluation and change, and to adjustment if necessary, based on the observations and recommendations of those who have been successful over time. Herein lies the key to better trader understanding and learning and, as a result, to profits.

Perhaps the single most important fact that endures throughout the lifetime of the trader is that much of what transpires in the stock and futures markets is totally unrelated to the systems or methods that have been chosen for the purpose of market timing. Even the most inexperienced speculators or investors soon discover that the emotional and psychological makeup of traders is more significant in the equation for success than is any single method of analysis, system or timing indicator. The millions of dollars (possibly billions) spent annually in the development of more effective timing techniques are, in the final analysis, wasted unless their costly conclusions can be translated into definitive market action in a consistent, disciplined fashion.

Successful Trading

Successful traders and investors are known to possess certain qualities that facilitate and enhance their achievements in the markets. While some may argue that these individuals were born to be successful, this is in fact not the case. More often than not, success is achieved by trial and error with few overnight rags-to-riches stories. Successful individuals in virtually any field will tell you that it took them years to be "overnight successes."

▲
——————————

Successful traders and investors are known to possess certain qualities that facilitate and enhance their achievements in the markets.

——————————
▼

Human behavior is so complex that determining which elements, behaviors or learning experiences are most important to achieving successful investing is exceptionally

2

Bernstein's Building Blocks to Success

During my years as a futures trader, I have made perhaps 10,000 to 15,000 trades in the markets. Yet I am still learning: Every trade is another lesson no matter how small that lesson may be; every trade is a challenge no matter how major or minor the task; and every trade is as likely to be a loss as it is a profit. It's not that I haven't learned a great deal as a trader, but rather that there is so much to learn, it makes what I have learned seem small in comparison.

Actually, only a few things must be *learned*, but literally thousands of behaviors must be *unlearned* if success is to follow. A trader can do many things wrong and so very few right! The trader must constantly watch for weaknesses and reflexive responses that inhibit success and ensure failure. Consequently, the relationship between the trader and the markets is a never-ending learning process. This has certainly been true in my case!

The Constant Struggle

˙I often wonder whether this fact of market life means that the skill of trading can never be totally learned or that the learning process will never end. For many years, I refused to accept the possibility that trading would be a lifelong struggle. I refused to admit that I must forever be on guard to avoid what Jesse Livermore called "the constant enemies struggling from within . . . fear and greed."

As I gained trading experience, I expected my task to become less difficult, more predictable, less anxiety-provoking, more tolerable and, above all, more profitable. However, I have learned through long, hard experience that this is not always true. *The process of becoming a successful trader is indeed without end*. No trader is immune to the possibility of a psychologically motivated error in judgment. No trader can constantly win, rarely lose or live his or her trading life in an eternal uptrend. Trading is a stepwise process that generally proceeds in a two-steps-forward, one-step-back fashion.

▲
_____

Trading is a stepwise process that generally proceeds in a two-steps-forward, one-step-back fashion.
_____
▼

Trials and Tribulations

If I were alone in my trials and tribulations as a trader, the pain of suffering failures would certainly be more intense and interpreted more personally. However, many traders find themselves in the significantly worse situation of being unable to profit consistently from their experiences in spite of "following all the rules." Unfortunately, most traders are not aware of the rules that lead to success, not disciplined enough to follow the rules if they know them or unable to understand why they lose when they lose. Herein rests the heart of the matter.

More to Futures than Expected

My education and experience as a clinical psychologist from 1968 through 1982 convinced me that there is more to futures trading and investing than any of us suspect, even those of us with years of experience in this venture. For all too many years, traders have wondered why there is such a disparity in trading results even among those who follow the same systems and methods. Why can two traders, each with the same amount of starting capital, the same basic trading philosophy and the same computer and/or quotation system, produce such markedly different results to the extent that one may win while the other may lose? The simple fact is undeniably: *Human behavior, as learned through life's myriad experiences, life's failures and successes, shapes attitudes and opinions, thereby mediating action.*

The ability to perceive market opportunities and, above all, to act upon such opportunities without the hindrance of psychological or behavioral restraints distinguishes winners from losers. Winners not only act differently than losers, but *the process that ultimately results in action is also distinctly different for winners than it is for losers.* Integral aspects of the process are such factors as perception, attitude, interpretation of reality as well as the ability to consistently formulate and implement plans.

Three Building Blocks

Although some traders will vehemently disagree with me, I have concluded that profitable trading and investing depend on the following three variables (not necessarily in order of importance):

1. **A trading system, method or indicator that has shown consistency and profitability both in historical back-testing and in real time for a significant length of time or for a significant number of trades.** A significant number of trades is defined as at least several hundred trades. A significant length of time is defined as at least five years and preferably five years in different types of markets (e.g., bull market, bear market, sideways market, etc.). Yet, as you will see from the interviews that follow, most recognized trading authorities place more emphasis on the trader than on the system. The system is important but not of primary significance.

2. **Discipline.** Discipline is the ability to formulate and plan, to implement that plan with nearly 100 percent consistency. I will discuss this aspect in great detail in Chapter 12.

3. **The ability to cope with losses.** Although winning in the market has its attendant demons, losing is a much greater evil. Losses are the precursors as well as the correlate of literally hundreds of potential trading blunders, not the least of which is the trader's unwillingness to follow the system that produced the losses. Because systems take time to perform, the trader who abandons a system often does so prematurely, frequently just before the system would have started to perform as it did in back-testing. Traders must work through losses without abandoning their system(s) if success is to follow.

The ability to integrate these variables into an overall response style or trading approach is ultimately what separates winning traders from losing traders. Other factors that fall under these three building block variables will be discussed in Chapters 11 and 12.

Different Scenarios

In addition to the importance of these three factors, their distribution in terms of weighting is also important. Consider the following three scenarios:

1. *A highly disciplined trader without an effective trading system.* Extremely profitable results rarely will be achieved (other than through chance). Although the discipline will be there, the truly great trades may not be entered due to the lack of an effective trading system.

2. *A trader who has developed, discovered or purchased an effective trading system but who lacks the all-important self-discipline variable.* In such a case, system performance will be either partially or totally denigrated, and the trader will find that his or her system, no matter how promising, is undermined by inconsistent and undisciplined application.

3. *A trader who not only has developed a trading system that meets the indicated criteria but also has achieved competence in the other two areas (self-discipline and the ability to cope with losses).* This is, of course, the best of all possible worlds for the trader and the most likely combination for consistent success as a trader.

My Story

My lifelong search to isolate, understand and remedy the factors that limit trader success has taken me in many directions. I have investigated thoroughly the teachings of traditional psychology and psychiatry as well as their contemporary offshoots. I have thoroughly studied the cognitive and learning theory approaches to human behavior and personality. My readings and experiences have taken me into the areas of new age psychology, self-realization, self-actualization, guided imagery, positive mental attitude, role playing and neurolinguistics. I have learned many lessons. My intention is to share them with you through the interviews and analyses in this book.

An "Overnight Success" in 20 Years

As a child, I was raised in a very poor family in Montreal, Canada. Speculating in the stock and futures markets was not only the furthest thing from my mind; it was the furthest thing from my ability—financially and educationally. When my academic career was about to end in my first year of high school due to poor scholarship, my family was fortunate enough to leave Montreal and to move to the northern suburbs of Chicago.

Within one week, my world was transformed. In Canada, I was raised on a street that was infested with gangs, violence and abject poverty. In the United States, specifically, Winnetka, Illinois, I was exposed to tremendous wealth, high society and unlimited opportunities. Although the move to the United States improved my family's financial resources considerably, they were never on a par with what was typical in my area.

As a high school student, I frequently was told by various friends that their fathers were "commodity traders." The term meant nothing to me other than what was plainly evident—the major trading families possessed tremendous wealth. Chicago, I soon learned, was the world capital of futures trading, the home of the Chicago Board of Trade and Chicago Mercantile Exchange, and a hotbed of trading family money.

Destiny

Although I did not know it at the time, my life was destined in the direction of futures trading. If anyone had told me that I would make my fortune in the futures markets, I would have looked at them in utter disbelief. Not only was I totally disinterested in stocks or futures; I had virtually no idea of what they actually were. But time has a way of changing things for people, and I have learned in my lifetime never to say never and never to say that my life will not go in a particular direction.

In my second year of college at the University of Illinois in Champaign, Illinois, as an undergraduate student in clinical psychology, I met John, a younger man whose father was an avid investor in stocks, futures and precious metals. Although the subject was of no interest to me, my friend's fervor intrigued me. For months he lectured me on the stock market, and for months his words made no impression on me. Yet John persisted in his efforts to recruit me as a trader, and ultimately his hard work paid off. I joined him in his market studies although, I admit, without his unique enthusiasm and verve.

The First Account

John convinced me to open a brokerage account so that we might invest in and trade gold mining shares. This was in the late 1960s when the gold and silver markets were in the infancy of their bullish moves. John himself was influenced by his father, a shrewd man who had survived the Depression and who had become prosperous in his own right by developing his skills as an independent investor. In those early days of my trading education, I failed to see the obvious similarities and sharp contrasts between father and son.

Today, however, with the aid of 20/20 hindsight, I see it all so clearly. John was highly technical in his approach. As a young investor, he was very excited about the technical approach to trading. He studied all the "right things": technical indicators, charts, earnings reports, government statistics and, of course, a plethora of investment newsletters. His reading was far-reaching and intense. John was capable of reciting the history of major market moves, the price trends of many stocks and the biographies of numerous legendary traders and investors.

John's father, on the other hand, was a quiet, methodical, almost compulsive individual who measured his words carefully. Through the years he had developed not only various highly precise attitudes about investing but had also developed a keen sense of patience and a marvelous perspective of economic history. While his son was aggressive, jumping in and out of quick-moving stocks, the father was slow and methodical. He accumulated large positions in stocks and precious metals, respected the importance of time and was clearly aware that the big money is made in the big pull.

Eggs, Eggs, Eggs

After my college days, I worked at a hospital treating chronically ill psychiatric patients. The work was difficult, the hours long and the rewards few and far between. At times, when I worked the midnight shift and the patients were finally in bed, there was little to do. On those peaceful occasions, I pursued my graduate studies, working on my masters thesis.

One fortuitous evening, I glanced at a copy of *Barron's*, which contained several advertisements for commodity brokerage firms. One particular ad attracted my attention. The ad discussed futures trading in shell eggs and boasted that egg prices were likely to skyrocket "to the moon" that year (1968). In those days of lax regulations and "wide open futures trading," ads could promise virtually anything with impunity. Unaware that I would soon be seduced by the markets, I wrote to the brokerage firm and requested more information.

Fast Talker—"Send Money!"

Soon thereafter Dan, a commodity broker, called and attempted to fast-talk me out of what little money I had. He dangled many carrots before my eyes, one of which was the promise that if I sent him $1,000, he could "make me a very rich man." In spite of my persistent refusal, Dan continued to call. I must admit that finally, after several weeks of badgering, I relented and agreed to send money. This was not an easy promise for me to make since I had virtually no money of my own. With loans from several friends, I raised the necessary $1,000 in capital to open an account.

After several days, statements began to arrive in the mail. "For your account and risk, we have bought today 1 September '68 shell egg." It was meaningless to me. All I knew was that within several weeks, my account had grown to approximately $2,500. My account partners were understandably nervous about this game. They decided to "cash out," leaving me with my share of the profits. My broker was unhappy but agreed to work with the small amount of money that was left, and he did so admirably. The money continued to grow. In fact, I was so impressed with what Dan was doing that I asked more questions and wondered whether this was something I could do on my own. Dan did not encourage me. He indicated to me that his approach to the market was seasonal, that his method of making money was based on weather forecasting. He continued to assert that "when chickens die, we get rich."

Roasting Chickens

Knowing that chickens are extremely sensitive to high temperatures and that their egg production rapidly declines as temperatures increase, Dan bought egg futures in advance of hot temperatures, hoping to capitalize on decreased supplies. Dan told me that when temperatures became even higher, "the chickens would roast and the price of eggs would go bananas." Indeed, he was right. I watched my account continue to grow as Dan traded egg contract upon egg contract for me, while the weather continued to heat up and the chickens roasted.

A Lesson in Greed

Before long, I fell victim to an ailment that, at one time or another, afflicts all futures traders—greed. It wasn't enough that Dan was earning me several hundred percent on my money. It wasn't enough that Dan was trading actively for me. And it wasn't enough that Dan was making all the decisions. I was convinced that what Dan was doing was easy. I felt that by reading a few books, I would soon be an expert trader. I was unaware that there was much more to trading than merely knowing what to trade. I was ignorant of the psychology of trading, the importance of trader emotion and the undermining forces of fear and greed. But I soon discovered them firsthand.

▲

... I fell victim to an ailment that,
at one time or another, afflicts all
futures traders—greed.

▼

Becoming a Statistic

For several weeks, I became an avid student of futures trading. I started with the classic text, *Modern Commodity Futures Trading* by Gerald Gold. After a few readings and several sample charts, I was convinced that I was an expert. After studying a pork belly chart, I decided that my next big move was going to be in the belly market. With trend lines on charts and a clear understanding that within the next several days my account would easily double in value, if not more, I confidently called Dan and asked him to buy pork bellies for me. Dan was flabbergasted that I would even think about trading pork bellies. "We know the egg market!" he exclaimed. "Don't you dare trade bellies, Jake; you'll lose your shirt," he warned. But I refused to listen to reason. I ordered Dan to buy me several pork belly contracts on the next morning's opening.

You can guess what happened next. Pork belly futures began to move limit down and "locked limit" several days in a row. The small fortune that Dan had made me was gone. When all was said and done, I had my original investment back plus $72. It was a sobering lesson. I called Dan for consolation. I will never forget his prophetic words. "Jake, I'll tell you where you went wrong. You couldn't leave well enough alone. We were doing so well. We had a system, we were trading that system and it wasn't enough for you. You had to get greedy. When we were making 500 percent, you wanted 1,000 percent. When we were making 1,000 percent, you wanted 10,000 percent. It just wasn't enough for you, was it? You just had to go and shoot for the moon. Jake, I've been in this business for only a few years, but I've seen it happen so many times. Traders go for broke, they never have enough and they don't know when to quit. Congratulations. You've just become a statistic!"

"What statistic is that?" I asked. "Jake, you've just joined the ranks of the 90 percent," he said dryly. Only then did I realize that I had joined the ranks of the 90 percent losers, that I too was a loser in spite of all Dan had done to make me a winner. But I knew that this would not be my last hurrah. I would be back.

The Aftermath

Determined to make my mark and my fortune as a futures trader, I embarked upon a two-year course of study. I read everything I could find on stock and futures trading. Slowly, almost imperceptibly, a pattern, which at first I refused to accept, emerged. Gradually I not only accepted it; I embraced it. Having been educated as a clinical psychologist, I was surprised at myself for not having recognized the connection sooner.

I realized that although it was important to approach the markets with an effective trading strategy, *the ultimate success or failure of a trader was not first and foremost a function of his or her trading system. It was rather a function of his or her personal psychology, that is, the ability to follow a program or system with discipline, consistency, persistence, self-control and self-confidence.* These important variables contribute either to the success or the failure of all trading systems.

The Psychological Puzzle

Gradually, the pieces of the psychological trading puzzle began to fall into place. I eventually realized that my many years of study in clinical psychology were, indeed, applicable to attaining my goal of being a successful futures trader. I recognized that everything in the markets was related to psychology and the self. I realized that trading systems were of secondary importance.

My life as a trader since then has been characterized by one psychological struggle after another, one small victory after another. The serious futures trader cannot totally avoid the trials and tribulations that must be encountered on the road to success. In some cases, these trials come quickly, and their lessons are learned quickly. But in far too many cases, mine included, lessons are learned slowly and painfully. Each loss, if not a strict function of our trading system, must be analyzed until its reasons are fully understood. This insight alone took me several years to achieve. However, now progress grows quickly, and success becomes more attainable.

What I have learned about futures trading will appear throughout the text of this book in the form of rules, realizations, insights and observations about the markets. You will also find my knowledge reflected in the interviews that follow. I sincerely wish and hope that the insights, attitudes and observations offered here will forever change your relationship with the markets for the better.

Though I have learned from each of my studies and experiences, the learning is still incomplete. Traders still commit the same blunders—blunders that inhibited their success for many years and will continue to do so unless they drastically change their personalities, response styles and relationship with the markets.

Opportunities for Victory

Today's traders are afforded numerous opportunities to improve their skills and emerge as victor in the battle for investment survival. Numerous treatment modalities for resolving dysfunctional behaviors exist; excellent courses and training seminars are designed to teach traders the skills they need to be consistently successful.

Yet, in spite of such general availability of courses and cures, the real world of trading has changed very little. Traders still lose, and traders still make the same mistakes. As an example, consider the sad but true fact that many traders continue to ride losses way beyond their predetermined stop loss point. They continue to do so repeatedly despite the fact that they have made the same mistakes for many years. These traders continue to err; they know they are wrong but cannot change.

▲
___

Traders still lose, and traders still make the same mistakes.

___
▼

If, at the very least, traders were making different efforts than they did 10 or 20 years ago, there might be a hint of progress. But, alas, this is not the case. This is truly unfortunate since it means that most traders will continue to contribute their funds to the small minority of successful traders who have control of their emotions and have mastered the skills necessary for success.

Although I do not offer what follows as a panacea for poor trading, I do feel that the insights and experiences that have been shared with me are sufficiently powerful and instructive to benefit every trader, whether aspiring novice or experienced professional. The market experts who agreed to participate in this project were open, honest and willing to share, in the hope that the lot of all traders might be improved.

It's Not Magic

I am not foolish enough to assume, for even an instant, that the trader's life will be transformed suddenly and magically after he or she reads this book. Positive changes do not happen overnight. We live in a world in which disorder is the norm. Great effort is required to overcome the entropy that pervades our daily lives. Most things, if left to themselves, will regress to a state of disorganization and disorder. Therefore, even armed with the insights that this book and others can provide, you will not achieve consistent success without effort. I do not therefore offer the insights in this book as the ultimate methods for improving your success.

Yet I feel strongly that if we can learn from those who have achieved success, in particular those who have been trading for many years, then we can use their knowledge and experience to our benefit. Remember, however, that *no matter how valuable the insights may be, they won't work for you unless you use them.*

The Key to Changing Negative Behaviors

As I stated earlier, there are many methods and courses that purport to teach traders how they can improve their results both in terms of profits and in terms of consistency. While many of them are promising and certainly effective for quite a few traders, they do not seem to answer all the important questions that must be answered if a trader is to succeed and remain successful over the long run. After years of study and trading, I have concluded that *perhaps the single best way to learn is to analyze and study the successes and failures*

of other traders, in particular, traders who have been successful and who have had, most importantly of all, a history of
longevity. I believe that the key to success is to learn from
these individuals.

▲

. . . perhaps the single best way to learn
is to analyze and study the successes and
failures of other traders . . .

▼

There are many ways in which we can go about achieving this goal. The most simple of these is, of course, to find
and read the writings of master traders, such as Jesse
Livermore, W.D. Gann, Arthur Cutten and others. This is
certainly a reasonable approach; however, I believe that a
more specific and contemporary technique may prove valid.
In particular, I am referring to the study and analysis of
attitudes, opinions and experiences of present-day market
analysts and traders.

3

George Angell

Experience Pays Off

George Angell has enjoyed many years of successful trading both on and off the floor. As an expert in short-term trading systems and futures spreads, he has shared his knowledge with others in books and videotapes. I first met George at an author's party given by one of my publishers. Soft spoken and shrewd, George has a keen wit and an observant nature. But his most obvious quality is perseverance. Like all good traders, George is not a quitter. Rather he persists until he attains his goal. Therein, I concluded, is one of George's greatest "secrets" to success.

A Biographical Sketch

George Angell is an ex-floor trader with more than 20 years of trading experience. He is one of the most recognized and well-respected authors in the futures industry. He has written seven books on futures investing, including *Real-Time Proven Commodity Spreads*, *How To Triple Your Money*

Every Year with Stock Index Futures and *Winning in the Commodities Market*. His most recent works are two videos: *The Essential Secrets of Day Trading* and *Advance Breakthroughs in Day Trading*.

An Interview with George Angell

What precipitated your desire to trade, and when?

It goes back a long way now. When I graduated from college, I got interested in options on stocks. And then I read about futures. I read Mort Schulman's book, *Anyone Can Make a Million*. This was back in the late '60s, early '70s, and when I learned about leverage and how it worked, I thought it was a good way to make money. From there, I started to dabble in the futures market, and I had the misfortune of being successful right away. So I thought it was easy. Later I realized it was a little bit more difficult, but I decided that I had to learn about it. I was living in Los Angeles at the time, and after a few years there, I decided to go to Chicago where I bought a seat. And from there I went to the floor, and that's where I got my real education.

What qualities do you feel contributed most to your success as a trader?

The quality would be: to be able to say that you are not always right—to be flexible and to admit mistakes.

Do you use specific techniques for coping with losses?

Yeah. First of all, I don't take any losses overnight—ever. Second of all, I try to keep them small. I don't use stops, but I watch it very closely so I'm out very quickly. The training as a floor trader helps with that.

Estimate what percentage of a trader's success is a direct result of a good system as opposed to trading skills. What would be the split?

The split would be—about 30 percent is the system, and 70 percent is the person using it. You could give the same system to two different people. One will be very successful with it, and one will have nothing but losses. You wouldn't think that would happen with a mechanical system, but it does. One reason is that one trader will watch it win seven times in a row, say, 'Oh, this is a great system' and start on the eighth day when it goes into a drawdown. Another reason is that a trader might be successful with it and decide to go from one lot to ten lots, and then he'll have losses on the ten lots trade. Discipline is very important.

Do you feel that close contact with the markets is necessary for success?

I do. I think you have to watch them closely. Sometimes you can get too close. I mean sometimes you are better *off* the floor than *in* the trading pit because you get carried away with emotion in the pit. Not that it's not a good training ground—it is.

Your recent book and videotape on day trading have established you as an authority in this area. What advice would you give to day traders regarding their emotions and success as a trader?

They have to learn to know themselves and not to get overly despondent when things go poorly or overly enthusiastic when things go well. So, again, it's controlling one's emotions and treating every day as a process so that a winning day and a losing day are more or less the same as just another day in the market where you know over time you'll come out ahead if you are doing the right thing.

Do you feel that your success was inspired by any famous traders?

I do. The people I met on the floor influenced me. When I first went to the floor, I met some people who were successful, and they kind of helped me along by telling me what to do and what not to do. So, if you can find a mentor in the market, it is a good idea, sure. If they teach you good lessons as you watch them trade, you see what they do. In general, though, people think it's a lot easier than it is.

Are you in touch with any specific experiences that either facilitated or inhibited your trading success?

Well, having money certainly helps. I mean, if you're trading on a shoestring, you worry about the money too much. What you have to do is separate yourself from the money so that you're thinking of the trade and not how much money you're making. That takes a certain amount of discipline that's hard to master, but it's very important to do if you're going to trade correctly.

What advice do you have for a new trader who seeks to achieve consistent success in the market?

You need a certain amount of money that's really risk capital so if you lose it all you can still feel like you can go on. It helps to know what you are doing, and most importantly it helps to have control over your emotions. You don't panic over losses and things like that.

If you had to do things all over again, knowing what you know now about trading, what would you do differently in regard to this business?

I would have started at a younger age. When I got out of college, I would have gone straight to the floor, gotten a job as a clerk and tried to apprentice myself with somebody who had been there. I didn't go to the floor until I was in my mid-30s, so I got a late start really. But you can do that only when you are ready to do it, and not everybody is at a very young age.

Analysis of George Angell's Interview

The Desire To Trade

Like many of the experts, George learned trading from the bottom up. After developing an interest in the markets and trading from the outside, he went to the trading floor and became an "insider." George's response points out the value of experience, particularly the experience one can acquire as a floor trader. Furthermore, he states, almost parenthetically, that he had the "misfortune" of being an instant success. Clearly, this shows that *the seasoned trader knows and appreciates the value of losses as learning experiences.*

Qualities Needed for Success

George's response here is a classic one indeed since it emphasizes the value of admitting to a mistake. This is yet another way of stating that one cannot ride losses. To ride a loss is to avoid admitting a mistake. And this can be very costly. George agrees therefore with most experts that *this is one of the worst blunders a trader can commit.* This also emphasizes the importance of being honest with yourself—a prerequisite to success as a trader and something so eloquently pointed out by Robert Prechter in his interview. Success as a trader, it seems, is more likely a function of *not* doing than doing.

Coping with Losses

George is in agreement with the other market masters. *Keep the losses small ... take them quickly* is the recurrent theme. In other words, the best way to cope with a loss is to limit it and to dispose of it quickly! His response echoes the "preservation of capital" theme that is prevalent throughout all the interviews.

A Good System Versus Trading Skills

According to George, success depends 30 percent on the system and 70 percent on the person using it. Give two people the same system; one will be successful, one will lose. This is an interesting response since George has developed a reputation in recent years as a seller of trading systems, books and videotapes designed to teach futures trading. Yet in spite of all that George knows about trading systems, he attributes 30 percent of the success factor to systems and 70 percent to the trader. I couldn't agree more.

Close Contact with the Markets

George underscores the importance of being in close touch with the market. This is understandable given his short-term trading orientation. But he warns us: . . . *sometimes you can get too close.*

Emotions—Asset or Liability?

George underscores the importance of emotional control, of knowing that each day—winning or losing—is part of the process of coming out ahead, if you are doing the right thing. This, by the way, is strikingly similar to Welles Wilder's response that it is important to do the "right thing" if we are to maximize profits and minimize losses.

Influenced by Famous Traders?

Like the other masters, George believes that his success was assisted markedly by fellow traders who had more experience than he did. Again, *the voice of experience ranks high on the list of valuable tools.* He tells us to follow the teachings of a mentor, and we will do well. I agree.

Experiences That Help or Hinder

While George's reply that *money certainly helps* is not exactly the answer I had hoped to hear, it is nevertheless a useful response since it emphasizes the value of being sufficiently capitalized. Too many traders begin with too little and lose it too fast. This is a sad but true fact of market life. He also refers to the value of not being attached to your money as an important aspect of discipline. You can't be too attached, too caring, too emotionally involved, or you will most certainly blunder!

Advice for the New Trader

This was yet another opportunity for George to reiterate his basic themes: (1) Start with enough capital, and (2) have control over your emotions if you want to increase your odds of success.

Hindsight

Given the opportunity, George would have started his career at an earlier age. This reinforces several points he (and other experts) have made: (1) Get more experience, and (2) follow a mentor or teacher.

Conclusion

George Angell's responses are concise and well thought out. He answered quickly, almost reflexively, which is the mark of experience. His many years of experience as a trader both on and off the floor attest to the validity of his responses and advice. George's responses are consistent with my own opinions and with the clear majority of the other market masters.

Gerald Appel

Overcoming Your Emotions

I met Gerald Appel in the mid-1980s when he and I spoke at several seminars. What impressed me most about Gerald was his dedication to the precise trading systems that he had developed for trading stock index futures. His techniques were precise, logical, well developed and appeared to have considerable validity from a technical standpoint.

Gerald appeared to be a highly disciplined trader as well as a very organized speaker. His methodology was extremely appealing due to its well-defined procedures and accompanying risk management procedures. In addition, Gerald had an obvious zest for his topic. He was dedicated to perfecting his methods.

A Biographical Sketch

Gerald Appel is president of Signalert Corporation and is an investment adviser, author and lecturer with an international reputation. He has written more than ten books on investment and stock market timing, as well as numerous monographs and articles that have appeared in such publications as *Barron's, Stocks & Commodities* and *Personal Finance*. In addition, Gerald has produced a number of investment videotapes related to investment tactics.

Two of Gerald's books have received the "Investment Book of the Year" award from the *Stock Trader's Almanac. Systems and Forecasts*, his newsletter that has been published since 1973, has been cited for its performance.

Gerald is a noted authority on stock and bond timing. He has appeared on "Wall Street Week with Louis Rukeyser" and is a regular guest on the various financial news networks. He participates in the *Mansfield Blue Ribbon* panel and provides an annual forecast for that charting publication. His market predictions appear frequently in *Barron's*.

An Interview with Gerald Appel

What precipitated your desire to trade, and when?

I guess I wanted to make money in the stock market. This was in 1965, 1966. It was more than 27 years ago.

What qualities do you feel contributed most to your success as a trader?

Well, I'm pretty disciplined and risk averse, you know. I think that's very important to keep the losses down and maintain kind of a disciplined, organized approach to trading. I'm quite good with numbers and statistics. I put a lot of research into the timing model that I use.

Do you use specific techniques for coping with losses?

Yes. Every trade has a fixed stop. You know, a stop loss built into the timing model that I use. All the models employ some sort of a trailing stop to protect profits.

Estimate what percentage of a trader's success is a direct result of a good system as opposed to trading skills. What would be the split?

Probably when a person refers to a trading system, he or she is referring to a system or method interpreted in an intuitive manner or to a totally mechanical trading system. In both cases, a person must follow the methods with as little emotional involvement as possible given that people are people. It's important to limit losses, to let profits run and to periodically evaluate performance. Trader and system are therefore equally important.

You are credited with having popularized the MACD, which has become by far one of the most widely followed timing indicators ever. Do you feel that traders have applied your timing methods consistently? If not, how would you rectify the situation?

I think that there are a lot of traders out there who are using the stuff that we've developed, including not just my MACD but a timing model called Time Trend 3 and a number of other timing tools. I know that there are people out there who are using it and using it very actively and very well. The big problem with people who don't use it is that they don't follow anything, which could be for a lot of reasons. Sometimes, any system might have a temporary period where it's not working too well. *People give up when a trade doesn't work out, and they give up on the system too quickly.* More often people begin tinkering with the system by injecting their own views or wishes about the stock market so that a system may say "buy," but they've decided for some other reason that the market is not going anywhere, so they act on their own. You know, they just don't follow it. *The biggest problem is people who try to use a system but sometimes do not follow it in a mechanical way. The whole idea of a system is to get the emotion out of the game.*

As a veteran trader of many years, what is the single most meaningful lesson you've learned?

Not to take small losses quickly, and do a lot of research into what I'm using before I use it. Once the research is in place, follow the things I develop.

Do you feel that your success was inspired by any famous traders? If so, who, and how so?

Not really. There still are people from whom I've learned, but not people who I would consider inspirational.

Are you in touch with any specific experiences that either facilitated or inhibited your trading success?

Not really. Most things you learn along the way. Most things you have to pay to learn. You take some losses, and that teaches you something. But I would say that the important thing is to try to keep moving and analyzing. When things begin to go wrong, first look at yourself and see if you are you doing anything differently. It has nothing to do with trading of the markets but how good you are feeling. But, you know, that aside, if you want to become good at it, first you should research and proceed and trade it on paper a while, and then use it. Periodically evaluate to see whether you are still performing well. But that's just after one of your trends.

Do you feel that emotion is an asset or a liability in successful trading?

By and large, it's a liability.

Can you elaborate on that?

Probably the biggest emotion that gets into trading is anxiety. And you become too fearful of losing or something like that. You know, you get out, you don't go in or something like that. The second emotion is connected with the need to feel like a winner, which often causes people to get out of their best positions too early and to keep their worst positions too long. But as a result of wanting to cash in their winnings and being afraid to take a loss or admit their mistakes, people gradually degrade their portfolios by holding onto the stocks that aren't performing well and getting into the stocks that are.

If you had to do things all over again, knowing what you know now about trading, what would you do differently in regard to this business?

Perhaps one thing I would do differently is to take more risks at different times than I sometimes do. You know, to the extent that my systems have been really quite efficient, I haven't always taken a winning position to some height. By and large, you know, I think we have done a good job for our clients. I hope to continue to do so.

Analysis of Gerald Appel's Interview

The Desire To Trade

Clearly, Gerald's motives were prompted by the desire to profit. His response was confident and terse, which is characteristic of successful traders.

Qualities Needed for Success

Gerald stresses four aspects that contributed to his success as a trader: *discipline, limiting losses, organization* and *research*. These are the four qualities that all the market masters interviewed for this book have emphasized to one degree or another.

Coping with Losses

Note the common thread in Gerald's response. His method for coping with losses is to use a fixed stop loss on each trade. The stop loss is a necessary part of the trading system as is the trailing stop loss. As you can see, Appel avoids the problems associated with riding losses by planning ahead. In this respect his response is very similar to those of the other experts. The key is to avoid the problem by planning ahead, by knowing what to do once there is a loss.

A Good System Versus Trading Skills

Clearly, Gerald favors the combination of a good system as well as a disciplined approach. Both are necessary for success.

Consistent Application of Your Timing Methods

Gerald says it all, concisely, precisely and with great accuracy! His response, which contains some of the most important issues in trading success, deserves repeating:

The big problem with people who don't use it is that they don't follow anything, which could be for a lot of reasons. Sometimes, any system might have a temporary period where it's not working too well. People give up when a trade doesn't work out, and they give up on the system too quickly. More often people begin tinkering with the system by injecting their own views or wishes about the stock market so that a system may say "buy," but they've decided for some other reason that the market is not going anywhere, so they act on their own. You know, they just don't follow it. The biggest problem is people who try to use a system but sometimes do not follow it in a mechanical way. The whole idea of a system is to get the emotion out of the game.

Influenced by Famous Traders?

For Gerald, the issue of inspiration apparently is unimportant. He seems to be a self-made trader and does not credit any famous traders with inspiring him to success.

Experiences That Help or Hinder

Although Gerald does not cite any specific experiences, he does elaborate on techniques that he uses to improve his success as a trader. Note the following excerpts from his response:

... when things begin to go wrong, first look at yourself and see if you are you doing anything differently. It has nothing to do with trading of the markets but how good you are feeling ... if you want to become good at it, first you should research and proceed and trade it on paper a while, and then use it. Periodically evaluate to see whether you are still performing well ....

Emotion—Asset or Liability?

Gerald's response is a simple statement that emotion is essentially a liability to the trader. In this respect, he agrees with all our experts: Emotion is one of the enemies, if not *the* chief enemy, of the trader. When asked to elaborate, Gerald makes the following statement, which succinctly summarizes his feelings:

... the biggest emotion that gets into trading is anxiety ... the second emotion is connected with the need to feel like a winner, which often causes people to get out of their best positions too early and to keep their worst positions too long. But that as a result of wanting to cash in their winnings and being afraid to take a loss or admit their mistakes, people gradually degrade their portfolios by holding on to the stocks that aren't performing well and getting into the stocks that are.

Hindsight

Gerald pats himself on the back for doing well but at the same time bemoans the fact that he may not have taken enough risk at times. He realizes that his conservatism has served him well. Risk is an individual matter that varies from trader to trader. There is no set standard. As long as risk is defined in dollar amounts, it ceases to be an issue unless the dollar risk is too high.

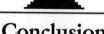

Conclusion

Gerald Appel is a highly disciplined, systematic trader. His methodology and discipline have brought him success. In many respects, he is a model trader whose attitudes and opinions should be studied thoroughly by all traders. His major ingredients for success are as follows:

- *Discipline.* Follow your trading system at all times.
- *Losses.* Limit losses by planning ahead.
- *Research.* Develop and refine effective trading systems.
- *Organization.* Plan ahead at all times in order to avoid errors.

5

Bruce Babcock

Tracking the Experts

Bruce Babcock is the futures industry "watchdog"—constantly monitoring the performance of advisory newsletters, hotlines and trading systems. In his role, Bruce has encountered literally hundreds, if not thousands, of trading systems, trading advisers and traders. This exposure has given Bruce a thorough education in what traders do to inhibit as well as to facilitate their success.

By nature, Bruce is a very analytical person. He is precise and deeply interested in understanding what makes things work and what makes them go astray. The precision and preparation required in his former profession as a trial attorney are clearly reflected in his attention to detail as a futures trader and publisher of *Commodity Traders Consumer Report*.

Since Bruce has seen traders come and go, he is sitting in the "catbird seat" when it comes to understanding the quintessential qualities for success. And his interview reflects this awareness. You may not like everything Bruce has to say—he is direct and unconcerned with sugarcoating his responses. But do pay attention to his comments since they emanate from a background of considerable experience.

Through the years, I have come to know Bruce well and to respect his opinions. I feel that if I need an objective opinion about either my own trading or that of others, or a reasonably unbiased analysis of systems, methods or indicators, I can call Bruce to solicit his input. I respect Bruce's ability to tell things as he really sees them. He has often told me things about myself and my trading that I haven't wanted to hear, but after considering his advice, I found a great deal of truth and direction in it.

Bruce is among the handful of traders whose work and professionalism I thoroughly respect.

A Biographical Sketch

Bruce Babcock grew up in New York and attended Yale University and the University of California at Berkeley. He received his bachelor's degree in business administration as well as a law degree. After a successful career as a federal prosecutor, he left his law office in 1979 at age 35 to concentrate on commodity trading.

Bruce has written six commodity trading books, including *The Business One Irwin Guide to Trading Systems* and *Trendiness in the Futures Markets*. He has had numerous articles published in *Futures* magazine and *Technical Analysis of Stocks and Commodities*. In 1983 Bruce started publishing *Commodity Traders Consumer Report*, a bimonthly newsletter that tracks the performance of the top commodity advisory services and makes a significant impact on the industry. He also publishes *Major Moves*, a long-term, special situation advisory letter. Bruce has designed numerous computer software programs for traders, including optimizable trading system programs, trading tools and a data management program for using continuous contracts.

Bruce's work has been featured in *The Wall Street Journal*, *Barron's*, *Forbes* and *Money* magazine. He has appeared frequently on the Financial News Network and is an occasional seminar sponsor and speaker.

An active commodity trader since 1975, Bruce continues to trade the markets for his own account and actively pursues his futures market research.

Interview with Bruce Babcock

What precipitated your desire to trade, and when?

In 1975, I changed stockbrokers. I was 32 years old at the time, single and a federal prosecutor by profession. My new broker thought my financial profile would allow me to speculate a little more. He suggested I trade some commodities. He told me that an associate in his office was a pretty good trader, that he would follow his ideas. I said, "Fine."

My first trade was in potatoes, although, truthfully, I can't remember whether I won or lost. Since I wanted to learn about how my money was being invested, I started reading about commodity trading. It became more and more fascinating. I soon opened an account with a specialized commodity broker and started calling my own shots.

What qualities do you feel contributed most to your success as a trader?

My natural aversion to risk and to gambling helped keep me from bankrupting myself while I learned how to trade. My skepticism, analytical ability and logical mind enabled me to sift through all the misinformation and discover the truth about profitable commodity trading. It took a very long time, however—over ten years.

Do you use specific techniques for coping with losses?

Yes. I have learned that I trade better when I isolate myself from my trading as much as possible.

Virtually all my trading is accomplished with computerized, mechanical systems. My own software, which I sell to the public, generates all the trading signals. By the way, I hold nothing back from my customers. I have no secret methods I keep to myself. Every system I use is available at a very reasonable price. Customers are free to trade exactly like I do.

My broker has a copy of my software programs. He runs the software himself, generates the trading signals and puts in the orders. Although we talk every once in a while, he can trade my systems on his own without any input from me.

When I am in town, I run my software myself and print out the signals to keep up with what is going on. When I travel, which I do frequently, I don't worry about my systems until I return.

I don't re-optimize or change my systems. Occasionally, I may add or delete a market from the portfolio that I trade. As my account increases, I may add new systems or additional contracts. I would allow myself to discard a system that does not perform, although I have not done this for three years.

Since I watch what goes on in the markets, I am aware of losses. But I don't dwell on how big they are or what is happening to the equity in my account. I try to follow the conventional wisdom—not to become too elated during good periods or too depressed during bad periods.

Estimate what percentage of a trader's success is a direct result of a good system as opposed to trading skills. What would be the split?

I am not sure exactly what you mean by this question. I see an ambiguity between someone who is using a system, yet at the same time applying "trading skills." If someone is trading with judgment, by my definition he is not using a system.

I will assume your successful trader is following a mechanical system. If that is the case, I suggest that one-third of his success would be the result of the quality of his system. One-third would be the result of his choice of markets to trade and keeping the size of his portfolio in line with his available capital. The remaining one-third would reflect his ability to trade the system religiously for a number of years. The correct choice of system and portfolio would give him a statistical advantage. The discipline to trade the system long enough would ensure that he could realize his statistical advantage.

How did your previous career as a trial attorney influence your skills as a trader . . . if at all?

This is a question I have never been asked before. I have thought carefully about the skills necessary to be a good trial lawyer. None of them except perhaps organizational ability seems useful for trading as I conduct it.

A good trial lawyer is well-organized. He can organize the facts of his case in a way that helps him easily retrieve them and explain the case to a jury that comes to the courthouse with no previous knowledge. A good trader is well-organized in the sense that he assembles the facts he needs to make proper trading decisions.

A good trial lawyer can think quickly "on his feet." He is able to respond to surprises. This may apply to those who trade with judgment but not to those like me who trade with a system.

A good trial lawyer has excellent common sense. This helps him evaluate the likely veracity of testimony and know how to counter it, if necessary. Common sense is not very useful for trading. What appears to make good sense is invariably wrong.

A good trial lawyer is a good speaker and a good actor. He can conceal his true feelings if necessary and make the case interesting for the judge or jury. Neither glibness nor acting ability will help a trader do anything but disguise or explain away his failures.

Finally, a good trial lawyer is persuasive. He knows how to present a case and argue its merits in a way that "pushes the right buttons" for the judge or jury. He is able to convince them to decide the case in his favor. This ability has no relevance to trading.

What do you feel is the single greatest skill a trader can possess or develop?

This is a difficult question. Obviously, there are a number of different skills that a trader needs in order to be successful. They are all important. If I had to pick just one that is most important, I would say it is the ability to perceive true reality.

Unsuccessful traders have a distorted view of the markets, themselves and what they are really doing when they trade. It is difficult for them to shed these misconceptions, so they are doomed to long-term failure.

The whole market universe is constructed in a way that reinforces their misconceptions. This compounds the challenge of overcoming them.

Do you feel that your success was inspired by any famous traders? If so, who, and how so?

Certainly, I learned many things from the famous traders whom I have known and whose work I have read over the years. However, I can't think of a single famous trader who trades like I do. Nor was there any famous person who inspired me to start trading or keep trading after an unsuccessful period. Thus, it would be hard for me to single out any one person as having inspired my success.

Are you in touch with any specific experiences that either facilitated or inhibited your trading success?

I can recall two especially large losing experiences. Both involved trading without a stop.

In one case, I was trading the yield curve with T-bill spreads. They were at an all-time historically low level, so I kept averaging down. Eventually, I gave up and took a huge loss. This taught me, I hope, never to average down and never to bank on historical price extremes as a barrier.

In the other case, I was holding a very large profitable position with a trailing stop loss to protect profits. I convinced myself to remove the stop loss without at least replacing it with another further away. The market made a historically large move in a short period of time and cost me a great deal of money. I learned from that never to trade without a stop in the market.

My learning process was evolutionary rather than revolutionary. Therefore, I can't really pinpoint any specific positive experiences that had a great influence on my progress. My first really big score was in the silver market in 1979 and 1980. At that point, I had quit law practice and was pursuing trading full-time. Those profits helped me continue my trading career.

As part of your business, you market trading systems. To what extent do you feel that a good trading system is important for success?

For many years, I have thought that the only chance a person has to be consistently profitable in the long term is to use a mechanical system. Only the most exceptional individuals have the ability consistently to overcome the emotional influences that prevent long-term profits. That was the underlying premise of my book, *The Dow Jones-Irwin Guide to Trading Systems*, now called *The Business One Irwin Guide to Trading Systems*.

Stated another way, it is virtually impossible to consistently trade with the trend, cut losses short and let profits run without depending on a mechanical system. Winning traders may not all use a computer to generate their entries and exits, but they probably use a mechanical system in their head.

The more a person trades without fixed rules, the less chance he or she has to be profitable over a multi-year period. Trading without fixed rules enhances the chances that a person will be trading with losing methods that over time give him or her a statistical disadvantage. Furthermore, trading without fixed rules allows emotional factors to influence trading decisions. This will usually result in bad decisions.

If you had to choose between discipline as a trader and a good trading system but could only choose one of these, which would it be, and why?

This is a false choice. If someone has a good trading system but no discipline, he or she will not follow that system. Having the system will be meaningless. If a trader has perfect discipline but no method to follow in a disciplined way, success will depend on luck.

If absolutely required to choose, I would choose the discipline to keep losses small. If a trader could do only that, he or she might stumble on enough winning trades to make some money. But I wouldn't bet on it.

Analysis of Bruce Babcock's Interview

Qualities Needed for Success

Clearly, Bruce favors the control of risk as a primary ingredient to success in futures trading. He points out the need to avoid the gambling impulse. Perhaps the most important aspect of his response is that he stresses the value of having an analytical and skeptical mind. As all traders know, there is a tremendous amount of misinformation in the futures arena. Literally hundreds of trading systems, methods and indicators exist, a vast majority of which do not work and never will. Bruce feels that the ability to separate the good from the bad, the profitable from the unprofitable, is a major asset on the road to success.

Coping with Losses

Isolation is the key to mastering futures trading according to Bruce. Here again, Bruce stresses the value of discipline, organization and a logical methodology to avoid the negative emotional consequences that accompany losses. He points out the value of having the assistance of a broker to help him manage his systems when he travels. The tone of Bruce's response appears somewhat unfeeling and insensitive. Yet I have known Bruce long enough to understand that he is anything but cold. This aspect of his trading personality is an asset. When it comes to futures trading, and in particular to implementing systems and dealing with losses, a trader must be somewhat unfeeling.

A Good System Versus Trading Skills

Here Bruce attributes one-third to the value of a system, one-third to the result of trading choices and one-third to the ability of a trader. He uses the word *religiously* in relation to the application of a trading system. His response leaves no doubt whatsoever that a system, if it is systematic, must be followed perfectly for it to succeed.

Applying Skills of an Attorney

As a trial attorney, Bruce was required to be organized and disciplined. Hence, his training in that field was excellent preparation for his career as a trader. Note, however, Bruce's statement that having common sense may be detrimental to the success of a trader. This is often the case. Often logic and scientific reasoning do not point the way to success. What works, works, because it works. It is not possible to predetermine whether a system will work or whether an indicator is any good. The test of its results will be the ultimate determinant of its value. Again we see the logic that is typical of Bruce Babcock.

Experiences That Help or Hinder

It has been said that traders often learn more from their losses than from their profits. Bruce confirms this assertion by discussing two of his worst losses. He notes that his learning process was *evolutionary*, namely it evolved from many experiences as opposed to specific experiences that "changed" his life.

Systems and Success

Bruce echoes the opinion of all the market masters interviewed. He points out the importance of a mechanical system whether it is computerized or not. The value of fixed rules is twofold. First, rules tell you what to do, and second and perhaps even more important, they help you maintain organization and discipline.

Discipline

Clearly, Bruce is in favor of maintaining a strong trading discipline as are all the market masters interviewed. *The essence of what Bruce says about discipline is that it must also be combined with a good trading system. Discipline alone will not make you a successful trader.*

Conclusion

Bruce Babcock has given us many valuable insights as to how traders can increase their odds for success. Given Bruce's years of experience both as trader and observer of other traders, his openness and willingness to share ideas with us was refreshing and appreciated. Bruce's pragmatic and performance-oriented thinking should serve as a lesson to all traders.

George Lane

Father of Stochastics

Known as the *father of stochastics* by many traders, George Lane's indicator is a household word among traders. I prefer, however, to think of George as the *granddaddy of futures trading*, the man with enough experiences and knowledge to easily fill ten volumes. It was therefore a distinct privilege and an honor to interview George.

Although I had known George professionally for many years, I had spent little time with him on a personal level. We have often exchanged expressions of mutual respect, I for George's development of his stochastic indicator, and he for my work with variations of his indicator.

George has enjoyed a long and varied career in virtually every facet of the futures industry. He is a survivor of all types of markets as well as a victor in the battle for trading success. He has had his ups and downs as we all have, yet he continues to emerge on top.

George was overjoyed to grant me the interview since he always has something to say and is always willing to share his point of view in the hope that others will benefit. Many years ago George was referred to as "crazy like a fox." Indeed he is just that. Behind his well-groomed white beard and cowboy hat are years of experience. Behind what some may once have considered worthless ideas about the futures markets is a man with a great depth of self-understanding, a man with significant market knowledge, a man who is both shrewd and calculating when applying his wisdom to futures trading. George walks softly but carries a big stick when it comes to futures trading.

A Biographical Sketch

George Lane received his training in the investment field at the E.F. Hutton school in New York in 1953. Upon his return to Chicago, George became a professional trader. He joined the staff of Investment Educators, where he taught stock market seminars and commodity courses. He and his research groups have developed technical indicators for trading the markets and originated indicators, such as %K, %D and the stochastic process (Lane's Stochastics).

In 1963, George bought a seat on the Mid-America Commodity Exchange (then called the Chicago Open Board of Trade), and served on its board of directors in 1965. That same year he formed a partnership, Miller-Lane & Co. For 11 years George wrote a daily market letter for his firm. He retired from Miller-Lane in 1974.

In 1977, three former employees asked him to help build a new firm. Four years, 14 states and 47 branch offices later, George had taught thousands of farmers, ranchers and bankers how to use the futures markets as a profit-making tool.

Until 1984, George served as research director for a third brokerage firm. He has written four commodity trading courses and a book entitled *Using Stochastics, Cycles and RSI*. He has been published in *The Market Technicians Association Journal* and *Stocks & Commodities* and is featured regularly in

Consensus. He has been interviewed by *Futures*, Financial News Network and Channel 26 in Chicago. He has taught numerous workshops on technical analysis.

An Interview with George Lane

What precipitated your desire to trade, and when?

Well, I was working for E.F. Hutton, the stock market had died and I was wandering about town buying a tie and bumming around downtown. I wandered into a place and found a bunch of guys screaming and yelling and jumping around. It was the Chicago Open Board of Trade. I was fascinated; I sat there and watched. An older man came over and took me into the office and sold me a membership for $25. I was a member of a commodities exchange. I could come over there and trade. It was kind of an accident.

And you didn't know anything about it?

I didn't know it existed until that day. It was kind of quiet in those days. I think yearly range of the hottest commodity, which was corn at that time that first year that I traded, was 23 cents. So things were kind of quiet. Markets never moved more than a cent and a quarter a day, and that was kind of nice because the margin was almost nonexistent. I mean, you come in for $20 and put it in the cashier's cage and go out and trade 200,000 bushels of corn. There was no risk to the brokers, so the margin was very small.

What qualities do you feel contributed most to your success as a trader?

I was very lucky. When I got there, the average age of that exchange was about 85. They hadn't sold a membership for seven or eight years. The Board of Trade hadn't sold a membership for four or five years. After I arrived, things livened up. I was at the right place at the right time, and I learned the trade when it was quiet and easy and grew with the volatility of the exchange. I was just lucky.

We were teaching stock market courses at the time. The man I was working for advertised . . . we started teaching commodity courses . . . we advertised that if you'd come take my course, why we'd cut your commissions in half. Gee, the round-turn commissions in those days were only $2.50, and all he did was buy a whole bunch of memberships at the Mid-Am and then give them to the people who took the course. Well, here all of a sudden at the Mid-America, we sold 175 memberships that were lying dormant in the treasury. Nobody had even expressed an interest in them. That got the Board of Trade all excited, and they ran over there to find out what Mid-America was doing that day. All of a sudden a lot of young people came in. Those old-timers were pretty appreciative. We kind of saved the exchange, I guess. And they took me under their wing and helped. And so I had two or three old-timers, fellows who had never had a losing week in ten years.

So you really were lucky?

Yeah, and I was lucky. They said, "Kid, if you don't straighten out, you're not going to make it." And they took me aside and helped a lot. That's what you need when you first start in any business. Some old-timer has to help you out.

Do you use specific techniques for coping with losses?

We use very close stops. With 28 years on the floor trading, fairly short-term for 45 years, I don't keep positions long. That's because I was there on the floor. On the floor, if it goes against you a little bit, you're out. I learned early that we don't take very big losses. And even nowadays we only trade mostly intra-day and, like in currencies, our losses are limited to $60. So I think if you control your losses and make them small, you're bound to make money in commodities. The biggest error that you have in commodities is letting yourself have big losses. And even with trading the S&P now, we limit our losses to $225. We just don't take a trade where the risk is greater.

Estimate what percentage of a trader's success is a direct result of a good system as opposed to trading skills. What would be the split?

Over the years, we have learned some systems or trading skills from other people, and we developed a few of our own and adapted some to our own personalities. As far as I'm concerned, we have an approach or a system, and that is almost 100 percent of our success now.

You are credited with having popularized the stochastic indicator, which has become by far one of the most widely followed timing indicators ever. Do you feel that traders have applied your timing methods consistently? If not, then how would you rectify the situation?

Stochastics can be used by newcomers, amateurs and professionals who don't really 100 percent understand it, and it will still work to a certain extent. But stochastics is just a little bit more sophisticated than just taking a quick look at it. It's a good overbought and an oversold. So I'm spending my declining years teaching at a school here in this little country town where I live. We teach a five-hour course in stochastics so the people can learn its sophisticated nuances. When you get that down, why, it's a fantastic tool.

Is it easily understood?

Yes. I have had no trouble. It just takes oh, three and a half, four hours to go over all the details. Most everybody grabs it.

As a veteran trader of many years, what is the single most meaningful lesson you've learned?

Oh, boy. Patience. Patience and stop losses. Limit your losses, and have patience trading. Everybody thinks commodities are so fast and furious. Actually a lot of the times, like flying an airplane, you just sit there bored to death, then there's the stark-raving fear when the prop quits turning. And in commodities, it's the same way. You're bored hour after hour. Then all of a sudden something happens, and you must have the ability to take advantage of it.

Everyone wants to make a fast buck in a day.

That's wrong. It's absolutely wrong. I've seen thousands of kids do that. The real winner is the fellow who consistently makes money, who watches the market, studies it and takes mediocre and small profits.

Do you feel that your success was inspired by any famous traders? If so, who, and how so?

Richard Det has helped a lot. He taught some courses at Mid-America. It kind of straightened a lot of people out. He's a natural trader and, gosh, we studied everybody who we've ever read. Jake, you helped a lot. A lot of people have contributed to my education.

Are you in touch with any specific experiences that either facilitated or inhibited your trading success?

Yeah. One time I lost $85,000 one afternoon just because I got stubborn. And I was going to push the market. I learned on that day that it does not work. I was also very lucky—we got in on the bull side of that Russian grain deal. It took a fabulous fortune out of that market. And so I've learned that there are about five to eight big profitable markets a year. And if the person will just wait patiently and spend several hours every week studying the monthlies and the weeklies and the long-terms and get into these markets early, there are several times a year that an absolute fortune can be made. But it does require a tremendous amount of patience. Sometimes it takes months before a market gets going.

Do you feel that emotion is an asset or a liability in successful trading?

Emotion is a liability. You must control your emotions. I think that better traders don't have much emotion, or they just don't show it.

If you had to do things all over again, knowing what you know now about trading, what would you do differently in regard to this business?

I think I would take the money out of the markets. To make over a million dollars and to leave it in there and keep trading it, I think, is foolish. I would take it out and put it in investments and stock it away somewhere.

Analysis of George Lane's Interview

George is especially candid in his interview. I feel that his responses come straight from the heart. But that's not unusual for George, who I have always known to be a down-to-earth, "no-holds-barred" person.

The Desire To Trade

George "fell" into the futures markets by accident as did so many of us. In this respect, George's answer is not too different from other market expert's replies. George is truly a veteran trader. When he made his first futures trade market, volatility was so very small that margin requirements were extremely small as well. His longevity as a futures trader makes his responses more credible and valuable than if he had been a novice.

Qualities Needed for Success

At first, George seems to attribute his success to luck rather than his qualities. Yet he goes on to state that several seasoned traders took him under their wing. On further questioning, George again refers to the importance of getting help from an "old timer," a seasoned veteran, which, of course, now applies to George as well.

Coping with Losses

George offers the same sage advice as do most of our market masters: *Keep your losses small*. I totally agree. The best way to cope with a loss is to anticipate the loss and to keep it small. In so doing you will not have difficulty coping!

A Good System Versus Trading Skills

George's response indicates the voice of experience. He says that he adapts systems to "suit" his personality. In other words, he looks long and hard for systems that will fit his personality. This is yet another approach to discipline. If you find a system that fits your style, the system will be much easier to follow. George has fine-tuned this process, after many years, to the extent that he now considers it nearly 100 percent of his success. But remember, it took George many years to get to this point.

Consistent Application of Your Timing Methods

The stochastic indicator is truly an important tool if used consistently. Naturally, George wants to promote and teach stochastics since it is the tool with which he is most closely associated.

Most Meaningful Lesson

George's response concerning his greatest lesson echoes the opinion expressed almost unanimously by our experts: *Patience. Patience and stop losses.* And his advice is well taken. In response to my comment that everyone wants to make a fast buck in a day, George disagreed, almost vehemently. *The real winner is the fellow who consistently makes money and watches the market, studies it and takes mediocre and small profits.*

Influenced by Famous Traders?

I'm honored that George chose to mention my name in response to my query concerning who influenced him. The essence of George's response is that many helped him along the road. Learning how to be successful is very much an individual matter, as I've stated previously. Hence, each trader must find his or her own niche, teacher and system.

Experiences That Help or Hinder

George's response on experiences is a classic! He notes that his single most valuable lesson was a large loss. And he is not alone in his opinion. In fact, it bears repeating:

. . . I've learned that there are about five to eight big profitable markets a year. And if the person will just wait patiently and spend several hours every week studying the monthlies and the weeklies and the long-terms and get into these markets early, there are several times a year that an absolute fortune can be made. But it does require a tremendous amount of patience. Sometimes it takes months before a market gets going.

So you must exhibit patience and know your markets to recognize and take advantage of opportunities when they present themselves. Being stubborn can cost you huge losses.

Emotion—Asset or Liability?

Concerning emotion, George succinctly states that emotion is a liability. Clearly, this underscores the value of emotional self-control as one of the key ingredients to success. If you allow your emotions to control your thoughts, you will surely be a loser!

Hindsight

In my first book, *The Investor's Quotient*, I state that it is important to take money out of the markets whenever trading is profitable. There are two reasons for this strategy:

1. It is important to reward yourself for good performance.
2. It is important to build up a cash inventory that you may need in the future if you experience a drawdown that may require you to add funds to your account. George confirmed the value of this procedure in his response.

All in all, my interview with George Lane revealed few surprises. As a veteran of about half a century in futures trading, this "old timer" offers advice for all who seek success in futures trading. His years of experience in markets of all types are valuable to us. His recommendations, attitudes and opinions underscore the basic premises of this book.

Conclusion

As a veteran trader and analyst, George Lane ranks among the top authorities in his field. His interview reveals that he is also in touch with the experiences, psychological qualities and perceptions that facilitate trading success. Do not discount his point of view. Do not take lightly what George has learned in a lifetime of trading.

7

Conrad Leslie

Forecasts That Move Markets

I first met Conrad Leslie in the early 1970s after being exposed to—actually, subjected to the consequences of—his crop forecasts for a number of years. I say this because his crop reports, particularly during my early trading in the 1960s and 1970s, almost always resulted in substantial market moves subsequent to their release and often in anticipation of their release. Conrad's work not only deserves attention for its excellence in research but also for its ability to move markets.

As I recall, I first met Conrad Leslie when I was a speaker at a *Futures* magazine seminar in the 1970s, which he attended. After finishing the formal portion of my presentation I took questions from the audience. While most questions were the typical "what are gold prices going to do this year?" queries, one gentleman repeatedly asked direct, probing and challenging questions. Later I learned that this man was Conrad Leslie. He introduced himself; I was shaking the hand of a man who was the grain and soybean crop forecaster *sine qua non*. As we chatted briefly, I was taken by several aspects of his personality: First, he is a humble, reserved, unpretentious man. In spite of his longevity and respect in the industry, Conrad does not couch himself in haughty attitudes, conceit or self-importance. He is genuine and down-to-earth. He displays emotion, affection and respect for my time as well as that of others.

Second, Conrad is persistent. If his questions are not answered, he probes further. And third, he is highly motivated to learn. When I met this man, who is known as a *cornerstone of fundamental analysis*, he was learning about technical analysis. He confessed to his shortcomings and indicated two facts that he considered important in the markets in addition to fundamentals: technical analysis and trader psychology. Conrad has a *joie de vivre* that, when combined with his probing looks, incisive questions and strong motivation, presented an awesome picture.

We can learn much from Conrad Leslie's responses.

A Biographical Sketch

Conrad Leslie has been studying the future and the futures markets for more than 40 years. *The New York Times* identifies him as the country's most widely read private crop forecaster. *Reuters, Dow-Jones, United Press International* and other news services distribute his monthly soybean, corn and wheat production estimates to agribusiness people around the world.

Conrad is a member of the Chicago Board of Trade and president of The Leslie Analytical Organization. His market interpretations reflect many years of business experience as a commodity broker and futures market analyst with major New York Stock Exchange member firms.

Conrad's penetrating daily grain market observations and daily grain and livestock price forecasts are presented each morning to brokers and their clients through ADM Investor Services.

An Interview with Conrad Leslie

What precipitated your desire to trade, and when?

My original entry into the world and industries of finance began in 1949 when I graduated from Merrill Lynch's eighth New York training class to become a broker assigned to the Columbus, Ohio, office. Charles Merrill endowed all of us with the idea that capitalism is good and that it was time to join him in a crusade to bring capitalism from Wall Street to the "grass roots" of America. In the early 1950s, a 2.5-million-share day on the New York Stock Exchange was a big day as was a Dow Jones move from 210 to 212. It soon became apparent that the two-year or three-year wait for an earnings or dividend increase for a stock (company) was too long for my patience and not as great a mental challenge as that offered by the futures markets. There, price changes were created by the 12-month cycle of changing production and demand. (Incidentally, corn production then was 2.7 billion bushels versus 1992's 9.5 billion and soybeans 299 million then versus 2.2 billion now.) After service as the office's futures broker, I joined E.I. duPont & Co. in Chicago and issued daily market comments and chart interpretations to their branch offices. Just before Ross Perot bought them out, I moved to Bache & Co. and did the same work. But we felt the USDA was too slow in issuing its reports of first-of-the-month conditions on the tenth of the month and too reserved in its month-to-month changes. So we surveyed elevator managers (instead of farmers) and started issuing crop estimates for sounder analysis, for an identity and as a goodwill contribution to agribusiness decisions.

Because a good analyst can command excellent compensation, including a percentage of the gross commissions, and a market position can weaken the accuracy of his or her daily writings, trading has been secondary to me, even through the later period of our independent writings distributed by Thomson McKinnon and E.F. Hutton brokers. In addition, there was always the uncertainty of conflict with positions held by one's own clients. When I reached 65, I decided it was time to stop laying awake nights thinking about customers and the size of their positions, so the accounts were phased out to others. (Neither my customers nor I traded my crop reports.)

What qualities do you feel contributed most to your success as a trader?

Several qualities contributed to my success:

- ◆ The experience of having been a broker and observing the successes and the mistakes and weaknesses in trading techniques by customers.

- ◆ An early recognition that successful trading depends 75 percent on technical work and 25 percent on fundamental analysis.

- ◆ An understanding that 80 percent of the traders in the market at any one time are going to end up being wrong—and lose their money.

- ◆ Thus, an early knowledge that for success one must be prepared to leave the crowd.

Do you use specific techniques for coping with losses?

Learning to trade, of course, can cost as much as a college education or more. You must study the reasons why that position ended up with a loss. Then, try to blank that trade out of your thinking. *Be bold, always be bold.*

Also, one should not be involved in trading every day. The great big moves in a commodity market occur only during one out of every three or four years. The less important price moves each year last only for two months or so. If one misses the up-move, usually the same amount of money can be made twice as fast when the correction develops.

Estimate what percentage of a trader's success is a direct result of a good system as opposed to trading skills.

One must have a foundation for trading based on a good system, such as a moving average or the breaking of a two-week or four-week range, etc. Without such, a trader is adrift in a sea and surf without a compass for confidence in direction. Trading skills identify whether or not a trader's personality and past experiences in life will enable him or her to compete successfully with the competition of the speculative crowd and the current personality of the market.

Do you follow any specific trading rules?

My philosophy for trading has evolved from observing the trading done by brokerage house customers and from conversations with successful traders "in the pits." Here are my basic "bare bones" rules:

◆ *Restrict your market positions to those that are in keeping with sound, basic market fundamentals.* When season supplies are inadequate, relative to probable demand, trade only the long side of the market. When season supplies are excessive, trade only the short side. If one thinks the price level is correct, remain on the sidelines.

◆ *Never buck an established market trend.* The market may know more than you know. Give up an opinion before you give up your money. Don't sell an uptrend; don't buy a downtrend.

◆ *Recognize that the greatest difficulty in trading is in knowing when to liquidate.* Most everyone knows when price moves are starting, but the point to identify is when and where they have stopped.

◆ *Keep up-to-date price charts.* Successful traders believe that visual pictures are an additional way to see and evaluate price and identify market thinking.

◆ *Never establish a position in the market until you see the potential for a large profit as opposed to a small loss.*

◆ *Be prepared mentally to make several attempts at boarding a major price move.* A trader's major market approach should be that of carrying out probing attempts that will result in being on board during major price moves. Be prepared to take small losses. Avoid the common thought that to take a loss will reflect poorly on your IQ.

◆ *Do not trade too many commodities at any one time.* Some traders have so many irons in the fire that they are unable to devote a reasonable amount of attention to any one of them. Four or five are enough.

◆ *Do not attempt to trade in commodities about which statistical information is vague or difficult to obtain.* It is preferable to trade U.S. commodities.

◆ *Do not develop an overextended market position.* To take either an individual or total position larger than the risk or failure justifies is to invite disaster. Plungers trade rashly and with only temporary success. *When your greed exceeds your fear, you will self-destruct.*

◆ *Restrict your trading to commodities that consistently return profits.* Confine your trading to those commodities at which you are a success.

◆ *Direct your efforts toward capitalizing on major price moves if you transact business through brokerage firms.* Professional traders earn their livelihoods by capitalizing on hourly news developments. Anyone earning a living another way should not attempt to compete in this type of day-by-day trading.

◆ *Go with the market as it makes new highs or new lows.* The act itself indicates that a basic change is taking place. Though the reasons may not yet be clearly recognized by the public, they are of sufficient force to establish a new price record.

Do you feel that close contact with the markets is necessary for success?

Today we live in an instantaneous economy. Billions of dollars can be transferred in a minute. Money managers throughout the world are being paid to constantly monitor the news and make decisions in response. The large positions of the money managers each day result in violent volatility in futures and stocks and bonds. Price stability and orderly money flows are no longer created by conservative federal governments and their banks through their open-market activities. But the more things fly—the greater are the profit opportunities for the players. In effect, we are recreating the markets of the 1930s.

A major price move in bonds or yen or soybeans can develop in a ten-minute period and before public broker-age-house brokers can explain developments via the telephone to more than two or three of their clients. Constant surveillance is an important requirement for long-term success in today's sensitive and unstable markets.

Your reports often have a significant impact on the markets. Can you explain the psychology of how your reports have influenced traders or markets during the many years that they've been watched so closely?

The more lights that shine on an object, the clearer it can be seen by all. The more even the flow of market prices and their reactions, the sounder society's business decisions. In contrast to the USDA's farmer-based reports, our informational sources are elevator managers. They are the business people who are putting money on the barrel head to buy first the U.S. wheat crop, then the soybeans and then the corn. They have to judge how much space they will need to store each harvest, how much empty space they can rent out and how much money they will have to borrow from the banks. These requirements seem to me to create a great sensitivity to crop developments. Can a farmer really tell before harvest is complete whether or not his or her fields will yield 38 or 44 bushels of soybeans per acre?

Since we issued our first survey report in 1960, most every brokerage and agribusiness firm has started to issue reports in order to remain professional and competitive. Usually about two dozen estimates are available to the market prior to our report and the USDA's forecast. Such is good for the marketplace. It enables orderly price adjustments and reduces the surprises. Most of these competitive estimates, however, are based on the weekly state crop condition reports rather than survey. (These state reports may not always be accurate because they sometimes reflect responses from only 70 or 80 farmers. But it is better for the markets to have weekly state reports than just monthly estimates.)

Are you in touch with any specific experiences that either facilitated or inhibited your trading success?

Throughout the years and even today, I force myself to go to one or two seminars a year in order to know whether or not there are any new ideas or discoveries in analytical work. I think I owe such time to my readers and to the profession. Unfortunately, in recent years, most of these seem to me to be ego or money-grabbing sessions for the benefit of the speakers. Now I feel lucky if I can get one idea from four or five presentations. However, attendance does renew one's confidence in his or her present applications as well as in the observation that "there is very little new in the marketplace," acknowledging, of course, that the psychology and the personalities of modern markets are constantly new.

And such are today's mental challenges for all analysts and all traders.

What advice do you have for a new trader who seeks to achieve consistent success in the markets?

I would attend classes and seminars held by the exchanges and brokerage firms, colleges and industry groups. I would read the educational text books available from the exchanges. For stock and industry ratings, I would study *Investor's Business Daily*. I would study Murphy's book, *Technical Analysis of the Futures Markets*, and six or seven other books on charting, candlesticks and computer trading. I would read the books written by successful retired traders, such as Peter Lynch, etc. I would read one new book a month in order to determine if there was anything new under the sun and to broaden my vision.

It usually takes two or three years of hard work to know whether or not a new approach is worthy of long-term adoption and success. So much of the hype of today seems to me to be "tea leaf reading," so one must allocate his or her time to that which seems worthy. I still like MACDs, but Stochastics and RSIs and Market Profiles have been relegated back to secondary thermometers of some time interest. A basic exercise is that I still mark and read my own bar charts every night, even after all of the past experiences. Such enables me to more clearly appraise the force of the psychology directing each of the markets.

Recently, I have often been disappointed when I paid more than $500 to attend a seminar (or for information about a new system). One recent seminar presented an approach that compiles eight trade losses in a row. Another presented positive profit results before deductions for commissions. A large part of another's profit record was based on the 1987 price collapse.

New traders should not be shocked if they lose money during their first two years of trading experiences. They also should not become discouraged if their performance fails to match those monthly published fund results. They should keep in mind: When the industry's average performance is stated, the funds that fail each month are not listed, as far as I know.

As a brokerage house broker, I observed that many of the successful traders were those whose occupations were involved in a commodity industry—soybeans, soybean oil, mining, crude oil, sugar, cocoa, the meats, lumber, cotton, etc. Doctors and lawyers do not often become good traders.

In my judgment, looking back at 15-year and 20-year records of performance isn't of great value. What one really needs to give a system credence for consideration is its results during the years since 1987. Money managers change as do industries and governments and economic values. The people in this world and their requirements will double during the next 30 years.

If you had to do things all over again, knowing what you know now about trading, what would you do differently?

I would:

◆ Arrive at trading decisions based more strongly on moving averages and their signals.

◆ Become an intensive student of daily candlestick chart formations instead of just bar charts.

◆ Adopt one or two computer trading signals, and avoid months of confusion and uncertainty that can come from reliance on five or six.

◆ Study and become more proficient in the use of computers for obtaining faster research results.

◆ Establish both a futures and a stock mutual fund.

Analysis of Conrad Leslie's Interview

The Desire To Trade

Conrad's reply to this question differs markedly from that of the others interviewed simply because he considers himself to be a market analyst first and foremost. The most noteworthy aspect of his response is that he considers his trading activities and his recognition as a crop forecaster to be somewhat conflicting. In other words, he feels that he cannot trade and forecast crop conditions at the same time. Conrad adds parenthetically at the end of his response that neither he nor his clients traded his forecasts. What he means specifically is that neither he nor his clients took advantage of the fact that his reports would often cause sharp market moves. Few analysts can resist the temptation to take a position in the markets prior to the release of a report that will have a predictable impact. Conrad is to be commended for his ethics, which are a rare commodity indeed in the futures markets. His ethics make the rest of his responses more credible and add to the value of his observations.

Qualities Needed for Success

Conrad speaks out unequivocally in favor of being a *contrarian*. He emphasizes that the majority of traders are wrong and are therefore losers, a realization that inextricably leads him to the conclusion that *for success one must be prepared to leave the crowd.* Yet also contained in his response is a healthy respect for technical analysis in addition to fundamental analysis. Many readers will, I am sure, be surprised to find that Conrad Leslie, seen by many as the dean of fundamental analysis, weights technical analysis as being 75 percent of the formula for success! An important point is that observing the successes and failures of his customers led him to his successful position as a trader.

Therefore, for Conrad Leslie success consists of three elements:

1. Use a 75/25 mix of technical and fundamental analysis.
2. Learn from the errors of other traders.
3. Be a contrarian.

Coping with Losses

Conrad offers sage advice: *Be bold, always be bold.* He stresses the value of blanking losing trades out of your mind. In other words, he emphasizes the importance of knowing that losses are part of the tuition of trading but that we cannot allow them to influence our willingness to trade. His "be bold" credo is expressed extremely well and reflects the thinking of such traders as Larry Williams, Bob Prechter and George Lane who also point out the importance of having a positive attitude regardless of losses.

Conrad makes a point that few others have made. He notes that if you fail to participate in a bull move, the ensuing bear move will often have the same or greater potential and that money can be made in the bear move twice as fast as in the bull move. Few traders think this way. Consider the many times you've taken a loss and entirely written that market off for a few weeks or a few months. Think of the many times you've missed a move and totally ignored the market only to find that in your rejection of the market you have also missed a move in the opposite direction. Clearly, Conrad's thinking reflects the thought processes of a market professional with years of experience.

A Good System Versus Trading Skills

Conrad waxes poetic when he alludes to a trader without a good system as adrift at sea without direction or self-confidence. Because he does not indicate whether a good trading system or trader skill carries more weight, I sensed that he considered both trading system and trader skill to be of equal importance. I extracted from his response a reference to confidence. My impression is that Conrad considers a good trading system to be something that imparts confidence and direction to the trader. This point of view is shared by the other experts interviewed.

Conrad also points out that a simple trading system is best. I believe, as do many other traders, that complicated is not necessarily synonymous with profits when it comes to trading systems. He confirms this by referring to several very simple systems—systems that although simple have proven themselves to be profitable over the years.

Specific Trading Rules

Conrad shares his detailed list of trading rules with us. All his rules reflect both his experience as well as his deep thought. The common thread in his trading rules is philosophical rather than procedural. In other words, Conrad stresses a psychological orientation to the markets in preference to a technical orientation. While not all of his rules are applicable to the strictly technical trader, they all make sense both intellectually as well as behaviorally.

The Psychology of Reports

Conrad sounds philosophical in stating that his reports shed more light on the market, which helps to clarify the picture. Using elevator managers instead of farmers as sources for the surveys reveals more valuable information to traders and provides a basis for making sound business decisions. Conrad does seem to attribute much value to the effect his reports have on the markets immediately upon their release. Conrad is primarily a position trader. He is not as interested in short-term price swings as are many traders. As a result, he does not find it necessary to focus on the "morning after" reaction to his crop estimates.

Experiences That Help or Hinder

Conrad stresses that he is constantly attempting to learn new things about trading. Yet he finds that little new exists.

He merely learns what he has known all along: *Very little is new in the marketplace*. The French say *plus ca change, plus ca meme chose* (the more things change, the more they stay the same). In so stating, he reflects the feelings of many successful traders who de-emphasize the importance of new methods and emphasize the value of adhering to the basic psychological and behavioral principles of trading.

Advice for the New Trader

Conrad has many suggestions, most of which fall into several categories. First, he stresses the value of education and that a winning education as a trader takes time.

Second, he points out that simple basic indicators tend to work best, and he states some of his preferences.

Finally, he provides a few guidelines on what the new trader might do both in finding worthwhile information and in avoiding the pitfalls of futures trading.

Hindsight

Clearly, Conrad has learned his lessons and presents us with specific goals. Once again he stresses simplicity. Note that he wants to focus on one or two computer trading signals as opposed to reliance on five or six, which he feels create confusion and uncertainty. He stresses the use of candlestick charts and moving averages, both basic techniques that all traders can learn.

Conclusion

In all, Conrad Leslie's interview reveals the character of a man who has spent many years as a futures trader and market analyst. His view of futures trading can be summarized as follows:

1. A solid education as well as a continuing education in futures trading is essential for success.

2. It is important to trade with the market trend using simple, basic, time-tested and reliable indicators. Any attempt to complicate a trading system will likely result in failure.

3. A positive psychological orientation is an essential ingredient for success.

4. A contrarian attitude is vital to success.

5. A mix of fundamentals and technicals is the best methodological approach.

8

Robert Prechter

Riding the Elliott Wave

Bob Prechter has established himself as the preeminent authority on the work of R.N. Elliott. His studies, publications and public pronouncements on the *Elliott Wave* theory have gained him a well-deserved reputation.

In spite of the fact that many market students and analysts consider the Elliott Wave theory to be a matter of interpretation and subjectivity, the principles underlying the Wave are sound. Although I have always found the Elliott Wave difficult to learn, I do not consider the seeming subjectivity of Elliott Wave analysis to be detrimental or seriously limiting in terms of the method's underlying validity. Many approaches to market analysis and trading require a certain degree of subjectivity and, by their very nature, will never be fully mechanical.

I respect Bob's work as well as his dedication to the art and science of Elliott Wave analysis. Bob is one of the

greatest thinkers in the profession, "thinkers" on the philosophical as well as the intellectual plane. He is much more
than an "Elliott Wave person." He is dedicated to work,
family and personal development. Although my contacts
with Bob have been brief, his persona has emerged clearly
through his writings, and it is with great respect for a peer
that I publish and interpret Bob's interview.

A Biographical Sketch

Robert R. Prechter, founder and president of Elliott
Wave International, established his reputation in the 1980s
as one of the world's most successful analysts and market
timers. He has been acknowledged as "the world leader in
Elliott Wave interpretation" by The Securities Institute, "the
champion market forecaster" by *Fortune* magazine and "the
nation's foremost proponent of the Elliott Wave method of
forecasting" by *The New York Times*.

Bob has published *Elliott Wave Commentary* since 1976
and has written several books on market analysis. In 1984 he
set an all-time record in the United States Trading Championship by returning 444.4 percent in a monitored real-
money options account in the four-month contest period.
During the 1980s, his *Elliott Wave Theorist* publication twice
won *Timer Digest's* "Timer of the Year" and *Hard Money
Digest's* "Award of Excellence." In December 1989, Financial
News Network named him "Guru of the Decade." According to *The Hulbert Financial Digest*, the *Theorist* matched the
performance of the Wilshire 5000 over the ten-year period
ending December 31, 1992, while being exposed to market
risk only 50 percent of the time.

In 1990, Bob commenced a search for experienced, proven
Elliott Wave analysts to provide market commentary to
institutional customers around the world. He expanded successfully Elliott Wave International's services to include short-term, intermediate-term and long-term analysis
of all major currency, interest rate and stock markets around
the world.

Bob served ten years on the board of directors of the national Market Technicians Association and in 1990 was elected its president. He also serves on the board of directors of the Foundation for the Study of Cycles. Before starting out independently, Bob worked with the Merrill Lynch Market Analysis Department in New York as a Technical Market Specialist. He obtained his degree in psychology from Yale University in 1971.

For *Global Market Perspective*, Bob provides commentary for world stock markets, U.S. Treasury bonds, gold, the economy and social trends.

An Interview with Robert Prechter

What precipitated your desire to trade, and when?

What initially interested me in the market was quintupling my money in 16 months in gold stocks in the early 1970s on my father's advice. To this day, I've never bettered that gain in unleveraged investments.

What qualities contributed most to your success as a trader?

When I was successful, it was due to discipline, which usually means taking decisive action immediately when called for. When I've lost money, it's been because I didn't do that.

Do you use specific techniques for coping with losses?

The coping part comes before the loss. If you take a position large enough to inflict serious financial damage upon yourself, you are a loser going out of the gate. I try to cope with my losses beforehand, determining amount of risk in advance. It is important to be honest with yourself. Most people cope with losses by lying to others and sometimes even to themselves. If you can't be honest, you're probably not handling losses well.

Estimate what percentage of a trader's success is a direct result of a good system as opposed to trading skills. What would be the split?

In one sense, it's 50/50. That is to say, you need both to be successful, in an equal measure. However, a good system is far easier to come by. The conquest of human nature therefore makes the difference. Psychologically speaking then, trading skills are 100 percent responsible for a trader's success.

Do you feel that close contact with the markets is necessary for success?

This is not a trick question, but it has a trick answer. If you're not close enough to the markets, you lose money. If you're too close to the markets, you lose money twice as fast. You should be just as close to the markets as you need to be in order to monitor and protect your trade.

The intense public following that you have enjoyed for so many years has often precipitated large market swings. Some analysts have blamed you for causing these emotional responses. How would you answer your critics?

Critics who accuse market analysts of causing market swings are usually the same ones who accuse market analysts of missing market turns. The second accusation nullifies the first. In other words, the theory they propose is that a market analyst is so "powerful" that his or her utterances cause people to act and therefore make the market go in the direction he or she wants it to go. (It would certainly make an analyst's life easier if it were true!) If one accepts this theory, then one must accept that said analyst will never, ever be wrong. His or her influences can only grow. Obviously, there is no such animal. A single error disproves the theory. The conclusion that critics are trying to avoid reaching is that analysts whose pronouncements are often followed by market moves in the expected direction are good at their craft.

Do you feel that your success was inspired by any famous traders? If so, who, and how so?

None of the famous traders had any influence on me. My primary early influences were Richard Russell in the area of market analysis and Dick Diamond in the area of trading. Russell taught me that technical analysis was proper and reasonable. My friend Diamond taught me how to trade options.

Are you in touch with any specific experiences that either facilitated or inhibited your trading success?

Yes. I've told a few of those stories in speeches. There's a 45-minute discussion in videotape #9 of our Educational Video Series, if anyone is interested.

What advice do you have for a new trader who seeks to achieve consistent success in the markets?

1. Get a method, and satisfy yourself that it works before trading real money.
2. Trade small amounts of real money. Paper trading omits the emotional factor, which is precisely the obstacle to overcome. Using large amounts of money will bankrupt you early, which, while an excellent lesson, is rather painful.

If you had to do things all over again, knowing what you know now about trading, what would you do differently in regard to this business?

I've been successful trading only when I've focused on it. When I've traded occasionally on the side while running my business, I'm usually just tossing lunch money to the real professionals. So to answer your question, I wouldn't change anything I've done because I have profited enough (financially sometimes and educationally other times!) from it. However, if I wanted to make trading my business, I would drop all other professional activities and focus on it exclusively.

For several years now, you have removed yourself from public visibility. Has this been a help or a hindrance in your life as a trader?

It's been a great help in my life but irrelevant to whether I'm making money trading. I'm working just as hard as always, having transformed the business from a 20-person retail organization to a 50-person institutionally oriented one. I quit TV, radio, interviews and articles over four years ago (with two exceptions for *Barron's*). Dave Allman took over the airwaves for me and has done an excellent job. He has a terrific mind for details and is entertaining as well. However, I made a case in January (1993) that we would see major turns in the stock market, the bond market and precious metals in 1993, which is 13 years from the last major turning point year, 1980. So I might show up on TV once or twice.

Do you foresee a time when futures trading will be so highly computerized that emotional responses will cease to be significant forces in the markets?

No. First, I expect most derivative stock market products to be outlawed sometime during or shortly following the next major bear market. Second, and this applies to all futures markets, a lot of computer programs have emotional factors built in. Remember portfolio insurance? Its strategy was to sell more as the market declined, just like people in panic. Most trading systems include stop loss strategies, so in my opinion, to the same extent that the world of investors is divided into those who sell rallies and buy declines versus those who buy rallies and sell declines, this ratio will persist in computer programs, which of course are designed by people. Entries and stops will be triggered at points that the people would presumably have chosen anyway. Even today, you can often predict "emotional" days by observing times when the market is about to break a 40-week moving average, which many computerized strategies employ as a trigger point. As new programmers try to anticipate that by triggering action earlier or to scalp in the opposite direction, etc., the same market action that would have existed otherwise will ultimately emerge.

You are the pre-eminent Elliott Wave authority in the world. Do you feel that human psychological response is to any extent a casual factor in the Wave theory?

My opinion is far more radical than that. Market psychology is not *responsive*. It is not the result of events outside the market. It is *impulsive, self-generating, self-sustaining* and *self-reversing*. The dynamics of social psychology operate in the same patterns over and over again, regardless of different attendant historical or cultural specifics. Events that make history are the *result* of the mass mental state that develops. This is the only possible explanation for the constancy of structure and consistency of patterns that markets reveal. The fact that markets follow the Wave Principle, as opposed to some other law, provides the added insight that social mood, and its result, history, follow the same law of pattern found throughout nature in other processes of growth and decay. That's what makes the subject more engaging than, say, the put/call ratio.

Analysis of Robert Prechter's Interview

The Desire To Trade

Bob's response concerning what attracted him to trade is not unusual in terms of what normally attracts traders to the markets. The ability to quintuple his money in 16 months attracted him to the markets. It's interesting to note that since his original big score in the gold market, Bob has been unable to better such gains in unleveraged investments. I have found that this situation is not unusual.

Frequently, a trader who is not knowledgeable about the markets will show better results than a seasoned veteran. Perhaps this is because many veteran traders have "too much knowledge" and tend to overthink their trades.

Qualities Needed for Success

Characteristic of traders who have been and continue to be successful, Bob's success is due to discipline. To his way of thinking, this means taking *immediate, decisive action*. This is perhaps one of the most cogent and valuable statements in the interview. Bob states that he lost money because he did not take immediate, decisive action. I cannot overemphasize the importance of taking immediate decisive action as a critically important variable in the formula for success whether trading, speculating or investing.

Coping with Losses

Bob claims that the most appropriate action to take in terms of coping with losses must be taken prior to the loss. It is absolutely true and unfortunately all too common that traders take positions that are much too large—big enough to inflict serious financial damage—and are therefore emotionally involved with their trades to a much greater degree than necessary. As Bob so appropriately puts it: *I try to cope with my losses beforehand, determining an appropriate amount of risk in advance.* Bob further states that it is important *to be honest with yourself.*

Perhaps this is the single most significant aspect of coping with losses. Unfortunately, many traders have never been honest with themselves and are unable to admit that they have a loss or that the position they're attempting to establish could easily lead to a loss—frequently a loss much larger than they should be willing to take. Therefore, losses must be anticipated and kept as small as possible, most certainly within the scope of what the trader can afford. Bob concludes: *If you can't be honest, you're probably not handling losses well.*

Bob's point is extremely important since it suggests strongly that the best offense is a strong defense. In other words, the best way to cope with losses is to be prepared for them, and to be prepared for losses, it is best to deal with losses that are manageable as opposed to losses that promote highly emotional responses, which in most cases are bound to be incorrect responses.

A Good System Versus Trading Skills

Bob feels that both a good system and trading skills are required in equal measure for success and that a good trading system is far easier to come by than is a trading discipline or trading skills. Perhaps his most telling comment is: *The conquest of human nature therefore makes the difference.*

Bob claims that, psychologically speaking, trading skills are responsible for a trader's success. I couldn't agree more; in fact, I find that this is a common thread underlying all the interviews. Trading systems are very important. However, trading systems must be implemented; and unless done so in an effective fashion according to their rules, they will yield no success. Therefore, the psychological aspect, the ability of a trader to have discipline and develop proper and effective trading skills, is extremely important.

Close Contact with the Markets

Bob indicates that if an individual is too close to the markets, it is more likely that money will be lost twice as quickly than if distant from the markets. However, he also feels that it is important to be close to the market to a certain extent to watch your investments or your trades. For Bob, it appears to be a delicate balance. This is in contrast to some traders, such as Larry Williams, who feel that distance from the market is very important. I am more inclined to believe that distance is important. However, futures traders, for example, may need to maintain close contact with the market in terms of the limitations imposed by their trading systems or methods.

Influencing Market Swings

For many years, market analysts have speculated on whether Bob Prechter has been responsible for large market swings. Frequently, a market analyst such as Bob makes a statement about the markets, and the markets, if in a highly nervous condition, respond dramatically—frequently dropping or falling sharply.

Those who lose money in the ensuing market move are often quick to point the finger of blame at the market analyst who made the statement that purportedly caused the market move. Consider carefully Bob's answer. He suggests that *those critics who accuse analysts of causing market swings are often the same ones who accuse analysts of missing market turns.*

I think his answer is certainly appropriate. It strongly indicates, as I have suspected for years, that *markets move when they are ready to move and that the utterances of a prognosticator can stimulate the market but that a market will not move unless it is predisposed to do so as a function of its internal or underlying condition.*

Influenced by Famous Traders?

Bob attributes limited influence to famous traders; he credits Richard Russell in the area of market analysis and

Dick Diamond in the area of trading. The one aspect that I would point out from Bob's response is that Richard Russell is the foremost proponent of the Dow Theory. The Dow Theory is fairly specific and has detailed elements that are systematic and therefore promote trader discipline. Bob's work as an Elliott Wave theorist is also important since a certain amount of discipline is required to interpret the Elliott Waves. Possibly his success over the years has been a function of the necessary discipline imposed by his trading methodology.

Advice for the New Trader

I particularly like Bob's advice for the new trader who seeks to achieve consistent success in the markets. His recommendations to *get a method and satisfy yourself that it works before trading real money* and *trade small amounts of real money* are very valuable in that they stress both elements of trading. Bob suggests that traders need a good system, method or approach to trading and that they need to begin trading on a small scale before they expand their operations. Bob states that *paper trading omits the emotional factor, which is precisely the obstacle that one must overcome to be successful.* Therefore, using large amounts of money certainly is not indicated during the initial stages of trading. However, Bob's response includes both elements, which is similar to what our other masters tell us.

Hindsight

We can all learn from Bob's experience. Bob states: *I've been successful trading only when I've focused on it.* This is so important I can't possibly overemphasize the value of taking this response to heart. Bob says that when he was trading on the side while attempting to run his business, he was *usually just tossing lunch money to the real professionals.* That is an important observation. Many traders trade simply because they feel they ought to or want to *take a flier.* I believe that trading is a business and should be run as a business. If you study the responses of the market masters interviewed in this book as well as experts featured in other market books, you will find that professional traders who have achieved success approach trading as a business, not as a hobby or an adventure. This is one of the prerequisites to consistent success as a trader, whether in stocks, futures or options.

Most telling is Bob's final response: *If I wanted to make trading my business, I would drop all other professional activities and focus on it exclusively.* True, true, true!

Public Visibility

When Bob Prechter chose to remove himself from public visibility a number of years ago, questions were raised concerning his motivation. Was this a help or a hindrance in his life as a trader? Bob feels that it was a great help in his life but irrelevant to whether he makes money as a trader or not. He claims to be working just as hard and concentrating primarily on his business, which appears to have done well and practically doubled in size. Bob's response clearly indicates that he is pleased with his decision to remove himself from public visibility and that it has certainly been a great help to him in business.

Emotional Responses Versus Computers

Could futures trading become so highly computerized that emotional responses would cease to be significant forces in the markets? Bob's response, at least in terms of my expectations, is certainly predictable. And I agree with him. Essentially, he predicts that emotion will always be a part of the market as new programs attempt to anticipate the triggers for trader action and reaction and that these would ultimately emerge as the same market action that would have existed otherwise.

I believe, as do most of the experts interviewed, that emotion will always be an important force in the markets, whether stocks, futures or options, and that it can never be eliminated. Therefore, the lesson here is: *Emotion must be dealt with, understood and, most of all, mastered by the trader who seeks to achieve consistent success.*

Market Psychology

In response to the possibility of human psychology affecting the Wave theory, Bob states that market psychology is *impulsive, self-generating, self-sustaining and self-reversing.* He indicates that, from his experience, the importance of the Wave theory is that markets are emotional, that they do follow the same law or pattern found throughout nature. This, according to Bob's understanding, is the Wave principle. In other words, he feels that emotion is the underlying factor in market movements and that the Elliott Wave is a measure of market emotion as expressed in terms of prices. Bob's responses in this case are similar to those of our other analysts and experts. Again, this reinforces the point that market emotion and *market response to price are primary underlying forces that motivate market moves.*

Conclusion

Every trader, novice or professional, can learn a great deal from the Robert Prechter interview. Bob is a deep thinker, obviously very verbal and unafraid to express his opinions no matter how they may affect his readers or listeners. Bob's chief points are:

- Traders are often undermined by their own emotions.
- Emotion must be understood and mastered if success is to be achieved.
- Trading is a business and must be treated as such.
- Discipline is important to achieving lasting success.

Welles Wilder

The Man behind Delta and RSI

I first met Welles Wilder in 1980 when I was part of a group that toured the Far East and presented commodity trading seminars. Welles has his clean-cut appearance and quiet demeanor; he is a deep thinker. Yet somehow I feel that he is somewhat detached from the markets, perhaps by intent but primarily to remain emotionally insulated from its effects.

I recall fondly Welles's comments as he spoke in Hong Kong to a large group of aspiring traders. Teaching one of his systems and showing its outstanding results over a lengthy period of time, Welles digressed for a moment with a brief aside: *"This has been a fantastic system for the last seven years, but remember that trading systems somehow have the uncanny ability to stop working for a while after they've been*

taught." The precise explanation for this seemingly para-
doxical state of affairs bewildered me for many years until
one day, in a moment of insight, I realized that systems
always look good on paper. *Only when traders begin to use
them does their performance deteriorate. It is the human element
that debases systems.*

Best known for his work on trading systems and timing
methods, such as the *reverse point wave* and *relative strength
index* (RSI), Welles is a most accomplished systems-and-
timing-signal researcher who has prompted a number of
controversies throughout the years, particularly in relation
to his Delta Society. It is not my intention to delve into the
politics or controversies that have been part of the Delta
system; rather it is my intent to present a fair and positive
picture of Welles as I have come to know him and, of course,
to analyze and understand his experiences and qualities as
revealed through his interview.

A Biographical Sketch

Welles Wilder is known worldwide for his original work
in the field of technical trading and for introducing the
concept that all markets follow a unique order that is predictable. He has lectured at seminars in the U.S., Canada,
Asia and Europe. Articles about Welles have appeared in
such publications as *Forbes, Barron's, Futures* and *Stocks &
Commodities* magazine.

Welles has been the owner and CEO of Trend Research,
Ltd. (publishing and promoting), Delta Sciences, Inc. (sup-
ports the Delta Society), Americom Corporation (introducing broker), Wellex, Ltd. (advertising agency) and Wilder
Classics (collects and restores classic Packards). He has
written four books: *New Concepts in Technical Trading Systems, The Adam Theory of Markets, The Wisdom of the Ages in
Acquiring Wealth* and *The Delta Phenomenon.*

An Interview with Welles Wilder

What precipitated your desire to trade, and when?

In the beginning, I didn't have a desire to trade. I came to the futures market in search of a way to buy silver utilizing the greatest leverage. That was in 1970. When it became apparent that the same leverage was available in other markets, then I began to trade other markets also.

What qualities do you feel contributed most to your success as a trader?

Patience, tenacity and a realistic expectation of profit.

Do you use specific techniques for coping with losses?

Yes, I look at losses as a businessperson looks at expenses. Losses are the cost of doing business. A lot of small losses along with some large profits are not hard to deal with. They are the trader's business expenses. The best and only technique I use to control losses is to simply decide before entering the trade how much I am willing to lose on that trade. I put my stop in as soon as I get my order filled, and I change it only in favor of the trade. I will never, ever take a large loss.

Estimate what percentage of a trader's success is a direct result of a good system as opposed to trading skills. What would be the split?

I think it depends on whether the trading system is totally mechanical or whether it requires some subjective input. If totally mechanical, then the only skill involved is to follow the system. To do this requires a trading skill in a class by itself. Few traders have this skill, so I'll say 50 percent of a trader's success lies in his or her ability to follow the system.

If the system requires some subjective input, then I believe the split would be 75 percent for the trader and 25 percent for the system!

You have long maintained that the markets have "perfect order." This has been a source of confusion for some traders. Can you explain what you mean?

All freely traded markets have an innate "perfect order" that they follow all the time. I call this the Delta Phenomenon. There are five time frames to the Delta order. This order works the same way for each market on all time frames. For example, consider the intermediate-term time frame. In this time frame, all markets repeat every four lunar months. This is about every 112 days. Within this 112-day period, each market has its own number of turning points in the series. Soybeans have the most turning points at 12. Crude oil has the least number of turning points at 7. The rotation of the turning points may change at point 1 when a new series begins, but once established at point 2, the high/low rotation will continue until the end of that series.

The "perfect order" comes from the fact that this order never changes. For instance, soybeans will always have 12 turning points in a high/low rotation every 112 days. Perfect order does not imply perfect accuracy. Let me explain. If you analyzed ten series of soybeans, you would learn that point 6 most often occurs on the 58th day of the series. If you took an average of all occurrences, you would find that sometimes the 6th point would come before the 58th day and sometimes after the 58th day. However, the average position in the series for point 6 would be the 58th day. Perfect order and perfect accuracy are two different things. If they were not, you would not be reading this!

What is the greatest lesson that you learned in your life as a trader?

The most valuable lesson is to always do the right thing in trading. W.D. Gann had 28 rules he always followed in trading. My book, *The Adam Theory of Markets,* stakes out the concept in 10 rules. If you follow Gann's 28 rules or the 10 rules, you will always do the right thing in trading. Doing the right thing doesn't guarantee you will make a profit because that depends on how good your system or trading method is. However, always doing the right thing does guarantee that in the long run you will always make the most money that your system or method is capable of making.

It also guarantees that you will lose the least amount of money when trading any system.

Do you feel that your success was inspired by any famous traders . . . if so, who, and how so?

When I first became interested in trading commodities, I collected everything I could get my hands on that involved technical trading. At the time, this meant renting works from several other collectors around the country. Frankly, I didn't understand anything about Gann except what was obvious. The Elliott Wave was intriguing but too nebulous for me to use.

Eventually, it came to me, as a mechanical engineer, that there was a void in the area of defining some basic concepts that could be used as building blocks to develop new trading concepts. For example, defining the concept of True Range led to the development of the Volatility system. The concept of Directional Movement led to the concept of defining a trending market. Defining the price relationship between two days (28 points of evaluation) precipitated the Swing Index Concept. I guess the bottom line is that, at that time, because of my engineering background, I felt more comfortable with mathematical market relationships than with things like chart trading techniques that required interpretation. To answer your question specifically, I can't think of any famous trader who inspired me.

Are you in touch with any specific experiences that either facilitated or inhibited your trading success?

Experience is a great teacher. I suppose that at one time or another, I have done everything wrong that could have been done wrong. In my early days, I wiped out my trading capital twice. Now that was an experience—one that will never, ever happen again. Absolute adherence to the 10 rules assures that. Talking about experiences, I must say that the greatest experience I have had regarding trading was the first time I saw the Delta order in the markets laid out on a chart with the colored lines and numbers so that I could see it immediately.

Do you have any favorite techniques for emotionally dealing with periods of drawdown?

If you are referring to trading a mechanical trading system, for me three things are involved. First, drawdowns must be accepted as an integral part of the trading process. Second, there must be a set limit to the percent of drawdown (based on the actual or historical experience) that will be accepted and still continue to trade. Third, with this in mind, go for it! It is out of your hands, your plan is in place and you don't have to worry about its being incumbent upon you to interfere with the process. The bad news is that you could lose a battle but not the war. The good news is that (assuming you know your system) the chances that you will lose the battle are highly unlikely.

What advice would you give to new traders interested in using some of your techniques?

I would give new traders the same advice that I would give anyone regardless of what techniques the trader is using. Learn to always do the right thing in trading before you take your first trade. W.D. Gann's 28 rules are in his book, *How To Make Profits in Commodities.* A free copy of the 10 rules is available by writing me (Cavida Ltd., PO Box 416, McLeansville, NC 27301).

Analysis of Welles Wilder's Interview

The Welles Wilder interview is especially interesting because Welles expresses his responses in a concise yet in-depth fashion. Welles's responses are in agreement with the responses of the other market masters interviewed.

The Desire To Trade

Leverage in the silver futures market attracted Welles to futures trading. This response is similar to those offered by the other market masters who were interviewed; he was interested in the profit potential.

Qualities Needed for Success

Welles believes that *patience, tenacity and a realistic expectation of profits* contributed most to his success as a trader. This very concise, direct response is completely consistent with what has previously been seen in the interviews. The common thread here is that patience and persistence are as important as the ability to anticipate reasonable profits and thereby avoid the greed, which is so common among new traders, particularly among traders who are not successful. It is important to have realistic expectations as well as the ability to persevere and to be patient in waiting for profits.

Coping with Losses

Welles indicates that he approaches trading much as a businessperson looks at the cost of doing business. The losses are therefore seen as a necessary part of trading. It is interesting to note that Welles, along with Bob Prechter, sees the importance of controlling losses as one of the most significant aspects of trading success. Before entering the trade, Welles determines how much he is willing to lose on that trade. Perhaps the most telling aspect of his response is: *I will never, ever take a large loss.* Neither will any of the other market masters.

It is important to understand the basic aspect of what Welles is saying about his trading. He indicates that losses are necessary, that losses will occur, *that losses must be kept small and that they must never be allowed to become unmanageably large.* This is one of the quintessential elements of success in trading and it pervades all our expert's opinions.

A Good System Versus Trading Skills

Welles indicates that if a system is totally mechanical, skill is required to a lesser degree than if it requires subjective input. However, he still estimates that 50 percent of a trader's success lies in the trader's ability to follow the system. In other words, Welles states: *To do this requires a trading skill in a class by itself.* Welles goes so far as to indicate that in the case of subjective systems, 75 percent of the formula for success involves the skill of the trader. Note here again the common thread that underlies all of our experts' responses, namely that skill is extremely important, much more so at times than is the value of the system itself.

An Explanation of "Perfect Order"

Through the years, Welles's long-debated statement about the "perfect order" has been the cause of considerable commentary, disagreement and confusion among traders. Thus this seemed an outstanding opportunity to ask Welles to respond to this issue. Welles's response is certainly reasonable and one that is echoed by all of the experts to one degree or another. *The greatest lesson to learn in the life of a trader is that the rules of trading must be followed if success is to be the result.*

Influenced by Famous Traders?

In response to the question about famous individuals who may have inspired Welles, the only one mentioned by name in Welles's response is W.D. Gann. However, it is interesting to note that Welles discusses his view of the market from the standpoint of a mechanical engineer and does not mention any particularly famous trader other than Gann as having been inspirational in his trading. I did not expect our experts to name so few inspirational individuals.

Experiences That Help or Hinder

In relation to experiences that either facilitated or inhibited his success as a trader, Welles responds that experience has been his greatest teacher. He indicates that, in his early days as a trader, *losing his trading capital twice was an invaluable experience* but one he will never repeat! In addition to his losing experiences in the markets, Welles notes that the order of the markets in terms of his Delta concept are important to his success as a trader.

Conclusion

Welles is a respected authority on futures trading as well as a seasoned trader. His engineering background has given him an appreciation for the technical approach to trading, yet he also values discipline and trader psychology. Welles's observations reinforce the other market masters' opinions.

Larry Williams

A Legend in His Time

I first met Larry Williams in the early 1970s. At the time I had just started my weekly commodity newsletter and noticed that Larry Williams's ad in *Commodities* magazine (now called *Futures*) purported to answer the question: Which commodity advisory service is best? I found the intent of the ad most intriguing since Larry was putting himself in the position of judging his competitors. I ordered the report. In spite of the fact that we were competitors in the advisory business, Larry evaluated my weekly newsletter very favorably.

When I telephoned Larry to thank him for his recommendation, he invited me to attend a commodity trading seminar that he was conducting in Chicago and to join him for breakfast before the seminar. I decided against wearing blue jeans (typical attire for me) and instead wore a suit, dress shoes and my best tie. The illustrious and world-renowned Larry Williams emerged from the elevator with shoulder-length hair and a sweatshirt. I was surprised but pleased to meet Larry the person, not Larry the icon.

As I listened to Larry's wonderful trading stories, I realized that he was very different from what I had imagined. A picture of Larry began to emerge that would soon teach me a significant lesson as a trader. The idea had not yet formed entirely in my mind, and it was not until that evening that the full concept was clear to me.

After breakfast I went to the seminar only to find that Larry's meeting had nothing to do with what I had expected. I had anticipated a seminar on trading techniques. Instead, he taught a host of psychological and personal development techniques gathered from many different sources, including Buddhism, self-psychology, Freudian psychology, positive motivation, visualization—in short, techniques that were well ahead of their time, techniques now recognized and accepted as part of the so-called new age movement. Larry's audience was either in love with, totally disinterested in or irate with the subject matter.

Some traders who had anticipated learning a trading system were disappointed. However, for those who stayed, great rewards followed. Larry was characteristically motivated, dynamic, positive and insightful. Those who listened carefully to what Larry had to say, participated in the exercises and accepted the new ideas, benefited.

Later that evening, Larry and I met for dinner in Chicago's Chinatown. He ordered a bottle of wine. The waiter replied that wine could be purchased only by the glass. Since the price of two glasses of wine was greater than the cost of an entire bottle, Larry insisted on ordering a bottle. The waiter replied that he was prohibited from selling wine by the bottle. Larry told the waiter that we would return shortly and asked me to accompany him to the nearest liquor store so he could buy a bottle of wine. Upon hearing this, the waiter replied that there were no liquor stores in Chinatown. Larry refused to accept his fate and told the waiter that we would be back shortly. We left the restaurant in search of a bottle. After being rejected at a number of bars, Larry's resolve increased. The issue was no longer that of acquiring a bottle of wine but rather *of beating the system.* One bar after another, Larry came out empty-handed until, on his 16th attempt Larry emerged victorious with bottle in hand.

Larry had accepted a challenge and beat the system. Suddenly the pieces of the puzzle fit together so neatly and so clearly. I saw what I had respected in Larry all along—his persistence. *Persistence* is the key to everything that Larry has achieved as a trader. Larry was not a quitter!

In my interview with Larry, I sought to tap into the qualities that Larry feels made him a successful trader many times over. Although Larry has been and will most likely continue to be one of the most controversial figures in the futures industry, his achievements exceed those of many other traders. Not only has Larry developed many highly profitable trading systems, but he has also introduced numerous innovative concepts to the futures industry. We can all learn from Larry's achievements as a trader and from his insightful point of view based on his experiences as a trader.

A Biographical Sketch

Larry Williams is one of the most widely quoted and followed investment advisers since the late 1960s. Articles about him have appeared in *Barron's, The Wall Street Journal, Forbes, Money* magazine and *Fortune.* He has made appearances on major television talk shows and is a contributing editor to the Financial News Network. He has been a speaker at leading commodity and economic conferences throughout the world.

Williams has written several books, including *The Secret of Selecting Stocks, How I Made One Million Dollars Trading Commodities, How Seasonal Factors Influence Commodities, How To Prosper in the Coming Good Years, The Definitive Guide to Futures Trading, Volumes I & II* and *The Mountain of Moses.*

An Interview with Larry Williams

What precipitated your desire to trade, and when?

Greed. It looked like easy money. That was in 1965.

What qualities do you feel contributed most to your success as a trader?

The ability to withstand pain, persevere, not give up and an insatiable desire to know more about what makes markets move.

Do you use specific techniques for coping with losses?

I just learned to accept them. That is part of this business. It goes with the turf; it happens to everybody; they're always going to be there. You just have to learn that that's the way it is and that while they're part of this business, you can't turn them off. You've got to learn to accept them. You can't turn them off. You can't let them get very big. You do have to have stop loss points; you have to make it mandatory to get out at a certain price level. But your stop is the more important aspect of managing your money. It doesn't have anything to do with the trade; it has to do with managing my money; exposing myself to ruin.

Estimate what percentage of a trader's success is a direct result of a good system as opposed to trading skills.

In my case, I don't think that I have any trading skills at all. So any success I have is through system.

What would be the split?

That's simple in my case. I don't think I'm a very good trader, and I think people who think they are good traders are under a delusion. That really comes back to bite them because they start swimming, get a winning streak of trade going, think it is themselves not their techniques and then make huge errors—something you would call *blowing out* in the marketplace.

Do you feel that close contact with the markets is necessary for success?

I don't know what you mean by the word *close*. If you mean looking at the market every 30 seconds or every hour, I don't think so, no. My contact with the market is daily. I may call a couple of times during the day to find out what's happening, to get a sense of what's happening, to hear the newest joke in Chicago, but I don't think that we should be hooked on each and every tick that prices take.

It is generally believed that you have made and lost fortunes in futures. If this is true, to what extent do you attribute each of these successes and failures?

Well, it is not true. After my first book, *How I Made a Million Dollars Trading Commodities*, 15, 20 years ago, there was a rumor that my next book would be *How I Lost a Million Dollars Trading Commodities*. I don't know where that rumor got started. I have made lots of money; I also have had losing time periods in the market. Like any trader, I've had a yo-yo effect in my life, but it hasn't gone from rags to riches to rags to riches to rags to riches.

Do you feel that your success was inspired by any famous traders? If so, who, and how so?

Well, I don't know about inspiration, but I did learn a good deal about fundamentals from a guy named Bill Meehan. In the stock market, I learned a lot about understanding the market from a fellow named Gil Haller. And over the years, I've talked a lot with Tom Demark.

All three of those people have certainly expanded my education and understanding of the market.

Are you in touch with any specific experiences that either facilitated or inhibited your trading success?

Let's go to the next question and come back to this one.

What advice do you have for a new trader who seeks to achieve consistent success in the markets?

My advice would be: Don't expect it. That's a false expectation. Consistent success is illusory. Success is here, but don't think it's going to happen each and every day or week or year. It's like a frog in the well; he jumps up three and flies down two and jumps up four and maybe flies down three. Don't have too high of expectations. Spend all of your money on education before you start trading because you're going to lose several thousands of dollars without knowing what you're doing. You better get educated first. Otherwise you'll lose the money and then figure out you can get educated, so you've got a double hit. Get your education first.

If you had to do things all over again, knowing what you know now about trading, what would you do differently in regard to this business?

Well, I would have used different stops from time to time, and I would have held on to some trades a lot longer than I did. I would have become knowledgeable about computers much earlier in my life. I wished I would have done that so I could have begun serious research earlier. I wished I would have learned more about money management earlier on and that I would have been a better person. I think a lot of being good in the market has to do with being a good person. I have a problem with that all the time, as I suspect we all do, but I try to be a whole individual with some interests other than making good in the market.

Are you in touch with any specific experiences that either facilitated or inhibited your trading success?

I think the inhibition of trading success comes from fear, and that comes from the experience of having done the wrong thing in the marketplace. So any inhibitions that I have about trading come from fear. You need to overcome fear—it is always there; it is not an ally; it is an enemy. The fearful experience still inhibits, i.e., losing money or getting into a quandary in the market. The most facilitating experience comes from research that shows me there are times that I have to take advantage of the market—absolute overwhelming advantages on my side of a trade. I still may make money on it, but the probability is the odds are scantily in my favor, and that comes from research. Experience has allowed me to do what I have done. Without research, I could never have taken $10,000 to $1.1 million when I won the Robbins World Cup Trade Championship or have turned a small amount of money into a million dollars when a million dollars meant something back in the late '60s. That was all based on understanding and research. To me, that's the most important experience in the market. It facilitates your success.

Analysis of Larry Williams's Interview

The Desire To Trade

Larry's response is direct, simple and honest. He tells it like it is. He trades for greed and greed alone. Although some traders enjoy the thrill or the challenge of trading, successful traders are interested primarily in the financial aspect of the game. Not one of our experts said that they like to trade for the challenge or "because it's there." They all began with an interest in making money. It's important to know why you trade and that your reason for trading is to make money and keep it.

Qualities Needed for Success

High on Larry's list of necessary qualities are the ability to withstand pain and perseverance. If Larry is not persistent, he is nothing. You will recall my brief story about Larry's persistence at the beginning of this chapter. Persistence and perseverance are essential aspects of the formula for trading success.

Coping with Losses

Larry does not offer any specific techniques for dealing with losses other than to state that losses are part of the game and, as a consequence, must be tolerated and accepted with as much self-control as possible. He stresses two elements for coping with losses, both of which are points made by the other experts interviewed. They are:

1. Keep the losses small.
2. Know ahead of time how much you are risking.

A Good System Versus Trading Skills

Now here's a typical "Larry Williams" answer; it required an additional prompt to evoke a lengthier response. Larry answers simply that he has no trading skills, that his success is entirely his system. In actuality, Larry is correct. A trader who can religiously follow his or her system is a trader who courts success. This is the trader's dream. The ability to follow a system totally and without thought is indeed what profitable trading is all about. Few traders can do this. Larry is evidently one who can. And so within his terse response is a wealth of information. Larry is simply saying that he is his systems and nothing more.

Concerning the split, Larry does elaborate somewhat by noting that traders often think they are better than their systems. When their systems work well, they think that it's due to their skill; when their systems fail to work well, the system is at fault. However, Larry's goal is to become one and the same with his systems, and this is the ultimate in mechanical trading. Naturally, if all hinges on the system, it had better be a good one!

Close Contact with the Markets

Larry indicates that he prefers to keep his distance from the markets. I know from personal communication with Larry that he does not have quotation equipment in his offices and that he prefers to avoid closely watching prices. He is the master of mechanical trading systems and as a result requires only limited inputs each day. While this approach works well for Larry, it will not necessarily suit all traders. On the whole, I think that traders are too close to the markets most of the time, and our experts tend to agree on this point.

The Key behind Fortunes Won and Lost

In his response, Larry denies the rumors and avoids the issue of what attributed to his success or failures. However, in examining his previous responses, I think that he more than answers this question.

Influenced by Famous Traders?

Larry credits much of his learning to three individuals—Bill Meehan, Gil Haller and Tom Demark. However, characteristically absent is credit to trading giants such as W.D. Gann or Jesse Livermore. This seems true for most of our experts. Perhaps heroes do not have heroes of their own!

Advice for the New Trader

Larry offers two important pieces of advice:

1. He suggests that education is important and that traders should get as much education as possible before they start trading.

2. He cautions us not to expect success because it is rare.

Both pieces of advice are valuable and correct.

Hindsight

Other than having used different stop losses from time to time, Larry underscores the importance of computer research and risk management, both of which he wishes he had ventured into earlier. He also stresses the importance of having interests outside of the market. In other words, being a well-rounded individual is an asset to successful trading.

Experiences That Help or Hinder

Larry stresses fear as an inhibiting force and research as a facilitating force. His advice bears repeating.

. . . the inhibition of trading success comes from fear and that comes from the experience of having done the wrong thing in the marketplace. So any inhibitions that I have about trading come from fear.

Conclusion

The interview with Larry went very much as expected. Larry displays his usual degree of seriousness combined with humor and disarming truth. Through his very basic and mechanical understanding of the markets, Larry has mastered self-discipline by having faith in his systems. He stresses the value of systems and their ability to facilitate self-confidence as a result of solid research.

The Keys to Success
as a Trader

On the whole, I felt that the interviews were extremely revealing on an individual basis. Although I had expected some agreement among our experts, I did not expect the agreement to be so significant and to be so similar across the board.

I imagine that the common elements among my panel of experts would also be similar for others who have been successful as traders in stock, futures and/or options markets. It is important to evaluate specifically what these elements are so that those who strive to achieve success in trading can learn from the experiences and comments of our experts. This chapter will review the qualities that our experts found to be important in the development of their trading success.

⅄ Patience

One important theme that underlies each interview is: *Patience is paramount if trading systems are to be effective.* The ability to wait for trades is very important since lack of patience frequently causes traders to take profits and losses too soon, thereby circumventing the value of their trading systems or methods.

Patience is important in the overall formula for success because most trading systems take time to work. The successful trader must be willing to await not only each individual trade but the trading system as a whole. As you know, it is not uncommon for trading systems to take a number of sequential losses before they begin to work. If a trader is impatient about waiting for the trading system to work, this will undermine the overall effectiveness of the program and thereby the success of the trader.

▲

Patience is paramount if trading systems are to be effective.

▼

Losses

Another theme that pervades the commentary of our experts is the importance of taking losses promptly and according to the system or method. Losses must be taken when the system indicates. And, as pointed out by the commentaries, losses must be kept to a minimum. While I do not wish to dwell on the obvious, it is important to realize that losses must be prepared for in advance, and once recognized, they must be cut short as quickly as possible. The trader who is following his or her trading system to the letter will be quick to take losses when they must be taken.

As Welles Wilder said, "doing the right things" is very important if a person wants to realize the largest profit and the smallest loss from the trading system.

▲
_____
*Losses must be taken when the
system indicates.*
_____
▼

Perseverance

Perseverance refers to the ability to persist with the trading system or method in spite of the fact that the system temporarily may not be functioning as expected. One of the single most important qualities for success that a trader can possess is the ability to persist and to persevere. All the experts agreed on the value of perseverance. Certainly this quality ranks uppermost in contributing to the success of a trader.

▲
_____
*One of the single most important
qualities for success . . . is the ability to
persist and to persevere.*
_____
▼

My Time-Tested Procedures

I cannot overemphasize that great traders are great because they have mastered the *discipline* of trading as well as its mechanical aspects. I've placed great emphasis on discipline. Since discipline is undoubtedly the weak link in the chain of trading behavior, consistent success is not possible without it. Various traders and writers offer distinctly different opinions on what constitutes discipline. My point of view has been tempered and shaped by more than 22 years of trading—trading that has exposed me to every conceivable type of market and news event. This has helped me develop a repertoire of time-tested procedures, which to one extent or another are echoed by the market masters I interviewed. Following are my time-tested procedures (not necessarily in order of importance).

Find Your Place

One of the most important considerations in futures trading is for the trader to find his or her place in the vast world of futures trading. A trader can do many things but only so many at one time. Find one or several techniques that you relate to and are confident about. Use these techniques in your trading, consistently, day in and day out. Determine which approaches suit you best, and consistently devote your time to those methods and for a reasonable period of time.

Don't Expect Immediate Results

Many a trader has been sorely disappointed when immediate success was not attainable. I urge you to persevere. Give yourself sufficient time to achieve success. It's one thing to learn how to ride a bicycle by reading a book (which is basically what we're doing here), yet it's a far different thing to actually get on that bicycle and ride it.

I assume that you have already done quite a bit of trading. While you may feel that this experience will serve you well, it will likely be detrimental since you come to the market with preconceived notions. You need to abandon these ideas in favor of those in this book. And remember that the process takes time.

Some failures are unavoidable. You will fall off the bicycle a few times before you can ride it. At first your progress will be shaky and slow, but after a while you will feel at home on the futures trading bicycle. It will take you where you choose to go, provided that you follow a smooth road. How long will it take? I cannot say exactly, perhaps more than two weeks and less than two years. Some individuals are successful in several weeks, whereas others cannot achieve consistent success as futures traders even after many years.

Keep Expectations to a Minimum

While some books on positive mental attitude tell you to have great expectations, I caution against it. Do not have great expectations. Expect to lose. Expect that with time you will begin to break even, in more time you will have profitable results. Expect that learning the game will cost you tuition both in terms of time and money. Hundreds, if not thousands, of traders have come to the markets with great expectations and a fistful of dollars but left the markets beaten, broke and broken. If anything, expect failure while hoping that through your efforts you can minimize the failures and maximize the successes.

Play Your Own Game

If you allow yourself to be exposed to and influenced by the many fantastic claims for ultimate trading systems and incredible seminars, you will be distracted on the road to success. While there is nothing wrong with improving on what you are doing, the act of searching, ever searching, tends to distract you from your goal. Don't be sidetracked from your goal. Persevere and ignore the claims.

The world of futures trading is constantly barraged by those claiming to have better systems, better methods, foolproof indicators, outstanding results and fail-safe methods. Before you give any new technique serious attention, make sure that what you're doing is not intrinsically better. Every system you test, every seminar you attend, every piece of software you buy and every path you take may prove to be a costly excursion away from your final destination. Systems take time, effort and money. *And these, my friends, are the most precious commodities in the world.* They are limited resources, not easily replaced. Therefore, I suggest that you find a methodology and commit to it for a predetermined length of time. And during this period of time *do not allow yourself to become distracted by anything else, even if it means that you need to close your eyes and ears to the magazines, newspapers and mail you receive.*

Admit to Your Losses

I have stated repeatedly throughout this book that *the single worst offense a trader can commit is to carry a loss beyond the point indicated by your system.* To do so is to violate the essence of futures trading and to risk exposure to everything that a futures trader seeks to avoid. *Do not, under any circumstances, violate this cardinal rule regardless of the excuse.*

If, perchance, you are "locked in" to a position due to a limit move against you, you have no choice. You could *spread a position off* (take an opposite position in a different contract month if possible) to avoid the exposure; however, there is still danger, even in a spread. In the event of a limit move in your favor, you may be tempted to hold your position overnight, expecting that there will be more profits in the morning. Even this is a dangerous procedure because *a limit move in either direction on any given day does not statistically guarantee follow-through in the same direction on the next day.* My research has shown that over the next several days there may be follow-through; however, what happens between now and then may wipe you out.

End the Day with a Profit

I encourage you to have one simple goal every day of your life as a futures trader: *Attempt to end the day with a profit.*

Place no dollar amount on the profit, or it may distract you. To set a goal too high would be unrealistic; to set a goal too low might be unfair. However, another type of goal—following your rules and being true to your methods—is the goal of the futures trader. If, however, you need to establish yourself a goal in terms of dollars, strive to end each day with at least a small profit.

Don't Let Good Profits Turn into Losses

Many a good trade has become a bad trade by turning a profit into a loss due to poor intra-day risk management. This is an important rule that you must not violate. Preservation of capital is quintessential to consistent success as a futures trader.

Don't Force Trades

Many traders crave action. This fatal flaw causes them to search out trading opportunities where and when none exist. If you have not seen an opportunity to trade and find yourself idly searching through your "screens" and charts for opportunities, you are headed for a disaster. *Do not attempt to create an opportunity where one does not exist.* Be patient. There will be trades tomorrow or the next day. The market always provides opportunities over time. *Do not ever, ever force yourself to trade if an opportunity is not readily apparent.*

Don't Hesitate

This is one of the worst enemies of the futures trader. The expression "those who hesitate have lost" relates more to the futures markets than anywhere else. Since futures trading is encapsulated in a circumscribed period of time, every moment you lose in entering or exiting a position may cost you money. If you hesitate, do so with premeditation and calculated caution. *Do not hesitate out of fear or indecision.* Hesitation subsequent to a clear-cut trading signal or opportunity indicates lack of confidence, and lack of confidence indicates that you are not comfortable with your choice of systems and/or methods or with your skills as a futures trader. Hesitation can be costly.

Keep a Diary

It will help you learn from your mistakes and, of course, from your successes. Refer to your diary both at the beginning of the new day and at the end of each trading day. *Learn from what you did the day before.*

If You Have To Watch the Markets and Cannot, Don't Trade

Some trading techniques are so mechanical that your presence is not required and live price quotes are not necessary. *Other methods, however, require your presence and close attention.* If a situation arises that requires you to leave your quote system, either close out your positions immediately or give your broker stop loss and/or other necessary orders. *Do not attempt to keep in touch with the markets by frequently calling for quotes or by using a portable quotation system.*

When in Doubt, Stay Out

This old expression is particularly appropriate for the futures trader. Not all indicators or signals will be clear all the time. Furthermore, other developments, such as news, reports or short-term fundamentals, make signals unclear or market response uncertain. In such cases, my best advice is to stay out—do not trade. There will always be plenty of trades; there is no need to enter a trade unless its potential outcome is relatively clear and free from the erratic influence of news or other fundamental events.

Do Your Homework

It never ceases to amaze me how few traders consistently do their market homework. Even though they have developed good market indicators and effective trading techniques, traders often fail to consistently keep up-to-date on the markets and allow a good methodology to turn into a bad one. This makes no sense. If you develop something that works, and if it is making money for you or facilitating your ability to make money, by all means continue with it.

Too many traders become complacent about their market studies, fail to do their homework and then wonder why they lose money. If you intend to succeed, you must do your homework no matter how simple or complex it may be.

Perhaps you have developed a trading system that requires no homework. This is certainly possible. Several of the techniques described in this book do not require homework. However, you still need to work on your trading diary and keep in close touch with trading opportunities that may develop during the next trading day. The only way to do this is to study the markets. This is what I mean by homework, and this is why it must be done.

Monitor Your Performance

Some traders refuse to monitor their trading results as a form of defense against being distressed by bad results. Avoid doing this. Always keep close track of your results on a trade-by-trade and day-by-day basis. Know where you stand at all times to acquire effective feedback about the techniques you are using. Unless you know where you stand, you will not have sufficient information about how well or how poorly your methods are performing. To keep track of your results, use a computerized accounting program or a manually updated spreadsheet. Pay close attention to your average winning trade and your average losing trade. Your average winners should be consistently larger than your average losers. If they are not, you are risking too much and getting too little. A change is needed.

Another good reason for keeping track of all your trades and their results is to determine if and when your trading technique, system or indicators have deteriorated and need change or review. Unless you check your performance, you will not know that change is necessary, other than perhaps a vague feeling that all is not going well.

More Complicated Is Not Necessarily More Profitable

You will be tempted to use more complicated trading systems. You may think, erroneously, that more rules will improve your system. You may feel that if your system considers more market variables, you will trade more profitably. My experience strongly suggests otherwise. With the exception of artificial-intelligence-based systems, which process vast amounts of data in exceedingly complex ways and relate this data to market patterns and relationships, adding new inputs or variables to your own analytical techniques does not necessarily improve them and may cause them to deteriorate.

If there is a relationship between complexity of system and profitability of system, it may well be an inverse relationship. *The simpler a system is, the more likely it is to be profitable.*

Beware of Market Myths

Markets are forever subject to the emotional influence of traders. Through the years, traders have believed that certain relationships exist in the markets *when these relationships do not exist at all.* Statistically, few consistent market relationships have persisted over many years. Do not get caught in the cycle of hope that perpetuates market myths.

Pyramid with Caution

Pyramiding is the act of adding increasingly larger units to your position as a market moves in your favor. You may begin by buying one unit and add two additional units once the trade has moved in your favor. If the trade continues to move in your favor, you may add four new units; if it continues in your favor, you might add six or eight units.

The essence of pyramiding is that *increasingly larger positions are added as the trade moves in your favor.* The upside of this methodology is that you accumulate a very large position consistent with the trend and use the capital available in open profits to margin new positions. The danger of pyramiding is that the pyramid is built upside down. It is heaviest at the top and rests on only one unit at the bottom. It is therefore subject to violent collapse at the slightest indication of a trend reversal. *If you intend to build a pyramid, do so by establishing your largest position first and follow it up by successively smaller numbers of units.*

Trade Only Active Markets

I'm repeating a bit of advice; however, I cannot stress it too strongly. By trading only in active markets, you avoid the problems that come with thinly traded markets and the relatively poor price executions that are so common in such markets. As a futures trader, you must have liquidity to move easily into and out of your positions without too much slippage. Moreover, if you intend to trade large positions, liquidity is absolutely essential for success. As a futures trader, you do not have time to wait for price executions to be reported to you, nor will you have time to go back and forth with different price orders in an effort to have your positions either entered or closed out.

Since markets wax and wane in terms of trading activity, you need to evaluate this on an ongoing basis to make certain that you are participating in actively traded markets. If you find yourself trading thin markets and experiencing the difficulties that go along with such markets, you can blame only yourself since you have violated one of the cardinal rules of futures trading.

As this book is being written, the active futures markets are as follows: S&P 500, Treasury bond, Swiss franc, Dmark, British pound, crude oil, Eurodollar and a handful of other futures markets. As you see, the number of vehicles open to the futures trader is rather small. But this, I assure you, is a blessing in disguise. An effective futures trader cannot spread him or herself too thin among too many choices.

Be a Contrarian

Some of the largest intra-day moves occur when they are least expected. The general trading public and most professionals will be on the wrong side of the market when these moves happen simply because they get blindsided by their collective sentiment. Mob psychology may be used to the advantage of the futures trader. If the market sentiment is heavily weighted on one side of the market or another, watch closely for timing indicators that will give you market entry on the opposite side of majority opinion.

Your Own Prerequisites to Success

Although these rules are important to remember if you sincerely want to be a successful futures trader, they are by no means the only prerequisites to success. Develop your own list based on your own experiences as a futures trader. The foregoing procedures, which appear to be supported by the market masters I interviewed, are merely a beginning, a base upon which to build your personal keys to success.

12

The Psychology of Trading

Perhaps the single most important aspect of any trading methodology, whether for the long-term, intermediate-term, short-term or day-trade, is the psychology of the trader. My work with trader psychology dates back to the first trade I ever made in 1968. Having been trained as a clinical psychologist, and having practiced as such for quite a few years, I am familiar with the limitations of the trader and the psychological roadblocks that traders constantly throw in their own paths. My book, *The Investor's Quotient*, continues to be a bestseller, which indicates that *traders realize their limitations and seek to know more about how to overcome them.*

While some people will disagree with me, I feel that this chapter is possibly the most important one in the entire book. While you may be tempted to skip this chapter, I sincerely believe that *to do so would be the worst mistake you could make*. Although it is impossible to completely cover this topic in one chapter, I will do my best to acquaint you with the pitfalls that await you as a futures trader. You would do well to consider my comments in relation to what the market masters have told us.

For many years, futures trading has been considered the most speculative of speculative trading activities. I believe that this is a market myth that has been perpetuated by those who are unable to trade profitably or who are afraid to do so. The fact of the matter is, the futures trader is in an advantageous position. The accomplished futures trader understands the limitations of what can be achieved as a speculator. The futures trader is like a sharpshooter. The futures trader is interested in finding the correct target, taking aim at it, pulling the trigger and bagging the prey. As mercenary as this may sound, this is what futures trading is all about. The effective futures trader keeps his or her powder dry, aims only at the most promising targets and aims only at targets that are likely to be hit. This is yet another point that was emphasized repeatedly by the masters.

The futures trader is interested in finding the correct target, taking aim at it, pulling the trigger and bagging the prey.

Qualities of a Successful Futures Trader

The futures trader must be consistent, efficient, adaptable and persistent. Because futures trading is unique among the many different avenues that are open to traders, it has its unique brand of psychology. In this chapter, I will acquaint you with the major issues that the futures trader faces and, moreover, suggest methods that you can use to overcome your limitations and maximize your strong points.

Trading Discipline

One aspect of universal agreement among the masters is the importance of *discipline*. This is probably the most worn-out term in futures trading. Saying the word is one thing; truly understanding its definition on an operational or behavioral level is another.

Discipline is not just the ability to develop a trading plan and to stay with it; it is also the ability to know when your plan is not working and therefore when to abandon it.

Discipline is the ability to give your futures trading positions sufficient time to work in your favor or, for that matter, sufficient time to work against you.

Discipline is the ability to trade again once you've taken a loss, to ignore extraneous information and to avoid inputs that are not related to the system you are using.

Discipline is the ability to maintain reasonable position size and to avoid the motion that leads to overtrading.

Discipline is the persistence required to maintain your trading systems and to calculate consistently the necessary timing indicators during the day, either manually or by computer.

Discipline, above all, is the ability to come back to the trading arena every day, regardless of whether you won, lost or broke even the day before.

As you can see, discipline consists of many different things. Discipline is not any one particular skill.

Discipline's Component Behaviors

Perhaps the best way to understand trading discipline is to examine some of its component behaviors.

Be Persistent

As I've said earlier, this is perhaps the single most important quality a trader can possess. Futures trading requires the ability to continue trading even when results have not been good. Due to the nature of markets and trading systems, good times frequently follow bad times, and bad times frequently follow good times. *Some of a trader's greatest successes occur following a string of losses.* This is why traders must be persistent in applying their trading methods and continue using them for a reasonable period of time. Consider the lessons learned from Larry Williams, George Lane and Conrad Leslie.

Futures trading requires the ability to continue trading even when results have not been good.

Individuals who quit too soon will not be in the markets when their systems begin to work; those who quit too late will run out of trading capital. Therefore, although persistence is important, it is also important to know when to quit and not play any longer using the existing system.

How do you develop persistence? While the answer appears simple, the implementation is not. You develop persistence by being persistent. While this may sound like a circular answer, it truly is not. *The only way to be persistent is to force yourself initially to do everything that must be done according to the dictates of your system or method.*

If you're having difficulty, try this. Make a commitment to a trading system or method. Follow through with that approach for a specific amount of time; take every trade according to the rules or, if the system is subjective, attempt to trade the system with as much consistency as possible. If you are consistent in applying your rules, in most cases you will have profits to show for your efforts. Even if your trading is not successful, you will have learned a great deal. You will have learned that you can follow a system or method, that you can trade in a disciplined fashion and, moreover, that the only way to do so is to be persistent by following as many of the trades and rules as possible.

Compare the above scenarios to the ignorance and confusion that come from haphazardly trading or inconsistently applying trading rules. Think back to your experiences as a trader. Remember your worst losing trades. You will find that *losses that were taken according to a system or method are easier to accept psychologically, whereas those that were not accepted according to the rules often turned into terrible monsters, ultimately costing you much, much more than they should have financially as well as psychologically.* To master the skill of persistence, you need to practice it. Make the commitment, and you will see some wonderful results, even over the short term.

Accept Losses

Another important quality that the market masters emphasized is the ability to accept losses and to take them promptly. Perhaps the single greatest downfall of all traders is the inability to take a loss when it should be taken. Losses have a nasty habit of becoming worse rather than better. Unless they are taken when they should be, the results will not be to your liking.

Although it is easier on one hand for the day trader to take a loss than it is for the position trader (since a loss must be accepted by the end of the trading day), it is still the downfall of many futures traders who are unwilling to accept the loss when it is a reasonable one. The good futures trader must have the ability to take a loss when the time to take that loss is right. What's right is dictated by the particular trading system or risk management technique you are using. From my experience and observations, *perhaps 75 percent or more of all large losses are due to not taking losses when they are small or relatively small or when they should be taken.*

The good futures trader must have the ability to take a loss when the time to take that loss is right.

I can certainly speak from experience when I say that my largest loss resulted from the fact that *I refused to take the loss when the time was right.* I allowed a $500 loss to turn into a $5,000 loss. Fortunately, that was the first and last time I was guilty of that serious a transgression. Unfortunately, many traders refuse to take losses when the time is right. The futures trader has two opportunities to take a loss. *The first opportunity is at the stop loss point as determined by a system or at the predetermined dollar risk stop. The second point is at the end of the day.*

Here are some suggestions as to how you can improve your ability to take losses when they should be taken:

◆ **Formulate your stop loss rules specifically whether they relate to systems or dollar risk amount, and type or write your rules in large print.** Place the hard copy close to your quotation equipment, the computer that you use for trading or the telephone from which you place your orders. If you do not use a computer or quotation system for your trades, keep your rules handy on an index card, and refer to them frequently during the day.

◆ **Make the commitment to accept completely your next ten losses as dictated by your system.** Once you have done this, the behavior will become habitual, and losses will be easier to accept.

◆ **If you trade with a full-service broker or a trading partner, make your broker or partner aware of where**

**your stop loss will be and have him or her remind you
that you must exit your position accordingly.** You may
also give your broker or partner the authority to do so for
you, if your relationship is close enough to allow for such
a procedure.

◆ **Place your stop loss as soon as your entry order has
been filled.** This procedure is much simpler although
one that I do not necessarily recommend at all times
because of the nature of futures trading.

Avoid Overtrading

Too many futures traders feel that they must trade every
day. Let's face it, some traders are addicted to trading. A day
without a trade for them is like a day without a meal. The fact
is that some days offer few if any trading opportunities. *The
futures trader who wishes to preserve capital and avoid losses as
well as unnecessary commission charges should understand that
futures trading is not an everyday event.* There will be days
when no trades are indicated. This is for the best.

▲
_____

*. . . futures trading is not an
everyday event.*
_____
▼

One of the telltale signs of the futures trader about to go
astray is the *searching-for-a-good-trade syndrome*. Have you
ever found yourself sitting at the computer or quotation
screen, bored because there were no trades that day? Have
you ever found your fingers idly rambling over the key-
board as you searched chart after chart for markets to trade?
This is the first sign of trouble. If you ever find yourself in this
position, *do yourself a favor and stop looking.* Good futures
trading opportunities do not occur every day.

Set standards as to which markets you will trade. If there are no trades in these markets, do not allow yourself to endlessly search for trades in obscure or thinly traded markets. This may work occasionally, but the odds of success are slim. The successful futures trader will specialize only in a handful of markets and will do well at these. Do not attempt to spread yourself too thin by looking for trading opportunities where they do not exist. This brings me to my next point.

Specialize

Successful futures trading is a time-consuming undertaking that requires close attention. Many of the market masters whom I interviewed specialized in certain markets or groups of markets. In most cases, successful trading requires diligence, follow-through and persistence. Because most trading techniques require close attention, traders should not be involved in too many markets at one time. I suggest that five to seven markets are sufficient for most traders. In fact, for new traders, I recommend specializing in one or two markets and attending to them thoroughly to develop your skills and increase your overall profits.

What should the new futures trader trade? Naturally, the answer to this question changes as a function of market conditions. Some markets are better to trade than others, for example, the currencies, S&P futures and Treasury bonds. However, other markets, such as silver, soybeans, the petroleum complex markets and other currencies, also make good futures trading vehicles under certain market conditions. Pay attention to any market that becomes active and volatile. For the newcomer I recommend a very limited portfolio of markets until techniques have been mastered and self-confidence has been achieved.

Begin with Sufficient Capital

Perhaps one of the worst blunders that any trader could commit, whether trading from the day time frame or from a position trade perspective, is to trade with insufficient capital. Virtually all the market masters agreed on this point. The argument may be made that the futures trader does not need to have substantial capital in his or her account since trades are closed out at the end of the day and therefore the necessity for sufficient margin to maintain positions is eliminated. While this may be true, those with limited funds cannot play the game as long as those with larger funds. In any venture it is important to start with sufficient capital so that the trader will not feel pressured to perform and can allow the particular trading system or methods sufficient opportunity to ride through periods of poor performance.

The trader with limited capital will be a nervous trader who looks to minimize losses beyond the point of realistic trading. Frequently, the anxious trader is knocked out of the game after a series of losses, before his or her trading methods have had the opportunity to perform. Consequently, capitalize your trading account sufficiently, or decide ahead of time that you will trade only a very limited portfolio consistent with your available capital. Do not start with an undercapitalized account. To begin trading with sufficient capital, the aspiring trader will have to be realistic and, above all, patient enough to gather the speculative capital that will be needed.

Use News to Your Advantage

Many a trader has learned the hard way that following the news frequently leads to losses. However, I have discovered ways in which the trader can use the fundamental news or developing international, domestic or political news to his or her advantage. *Do not be a follower of the news; rather "fade" the news.* Use the news to exit positions that you probably established before the news became public knowledge. I firmly believe in the old market dictum: *Buy on rumor, sell on news.* On an intra-day basis, markets are very sensitive to news well before the news is known by most traders. Insiders buy and sell on expectation, sometimes based on rumor, frequently based on fact. They establish positions before the general public is aware of the news; once the news has become public knowledge, they take advantage of the surge or the drop in prices to exit positions.

▲

Buy on rumor, sell on news.

▼

Therefore, to use the news to your advantage, you must be a contrarian. This is especially true from the futures trading perspective. While there is nothing wrong with following intra-day trends, frequently these trends react strongly to news developments. If you are following a valid trading system or method, you will most often be on the correct side of the market when such news develops. Take advantage of price surges or declines to exit your position. This requires self-control and the ability to see the news as your opportunity to get out, not as your opportunity to hold on for even more profit!

Take Advantage of Brief Price Surges

To trade profitably, you must also learn to take advantage of brief flurries in prices. At times, markets will drop or rally quickly, seemingly in response to no news. What may be happening is a rumor on the trading floor, a large buyer or buy order, or large seller or sell order of which you are unaware. Such brief price surges or drops are opportunities for you to exit positions consistent with the price move.

Regardless of the source, consider all price rallies or declines that occur quickly within the day's trading session as an opportunity for you either to exit your current position at a profit or to establish a new position using support and resistance methods that were outlined previously. It is important to develop this quality as a futures trader since it is entirely consistent with the futures trading objective.

Too many futures traders assume that bulges or sharp declines in price within the day are basically meaningless. Believe me, they're not. They are tailor-made for the futures trader. The futures trader who is committed to taking a profit out of the market every day must take advantage of these price moves. If you decide not to do so, you must either raise or lower your stop loss (depending on your position), or you must use an appropriate mental stop loss that is adjusted to the change in price. Simply, this means: Use a trailing stop loss in the event that the price move is negated shortly after it begins. In this way, you will have given yourself an opportunity to lock in a larger profit that you might not otherwise have had.

Stick to Your Goals

Above all, remember that *as a futures trader you have one major goal: to make money.* To do so, you must be particularly aware of your net profits at all times. My advice, which is based on many years of futures trading, is to set yourself specific standards and conditions under which you will begin to liquidate positions. My advice is to do so while the trend is still in your favor. You may either begin to close out your positions at that time or you may use a follow-up stop loss procedure to "lock in" existing profits.

▲
_____

. . . as a futures trader you have one major goal: to make money.

_____
▼

To achieve your goals, you need to internalize them and keep them foremost in your mind at all times. What is right and proper for the position trader or for the short-term trader is not necessarily good for the futures trader. If you find yourself wanting to ride profits or losses overnight, you are not being true to your goal as a futures trader. If you wish to day trade and position trade as well, I urge you to do so in different accounts to avoid confusion. Keep your goal in mind, and you will be less likely to stray from it.

Use Market Sentiment To Find Short-Term and Day-Trading Opportunities

I have already discussed the importance of going against the majority opinion to find profitable futures trading opportunities. *I believe that this is one of the most important qualities a futures trader can possess.* While there is certainly a great deal of money to be made in futures trading with the existing trend, *it is also important to know when the existing trend has reached a possible turning point.* One of the best ways, if not *the* best way of doing this, is through the use of market sentiment. Although I discussed the particulars of applying market sentiment for the purposes of futures trading, I want to stress its importance. *The futures trader must also be a contrarian.* This does not mean that you must buck the trend, but it does mean that *you must always be aware of whether sentiment is very high or very low.* This will give you important clues as to whether you should be quick to take profits, whether you can allow profits to run and whether you should look for trading opportunities on the opposite side of the existing trend.

My Conclusions about Trader Psychology

While there are many other qualities that a successful futures trader must either possess or acquire, these are the most significant ones. If you strive to develop these qualities, *your odds of success as a futures trader will certainly be better.* I have learned, after many years of trading, that *the major difference between those who are successful traders and those who are not is found in their psychological makeup and in the skills they have acquired as traders rather than in the trading systems they use.*

While it is certainly helpful to have an effective trading system, even the best trading system in the hands of an undisciplined trader is nothing more than a destructive tool. Consequently, you must develop your skills as a futures trader along the guidelines provided in this chapter.

Occasionally, traders have idiosyncratic difficulties in the markets that must be addressed on an individual basis. If this is the case, identify your particular problem as succinctly as you can. If you cannot formulate a good method for minimizing the problem that this behavior causes, contact a professional for assistance. If you are not successful in your search for help, please drop me a line. I may have some helpful suggestions for you.

Finally, I urge you to carefully study the words of the market masters. Take their observations and experiences seriously. Learn from their examples and insights. Your time will be well spent.

13

Conclusion

The process of writing this book has been particularly educational. I do indeed feel privileged to have had the opportunity to evaluate and analyze responses to these important questions from fellow traders and analysts whose work I have respected for many years.

While the process of conducting and analyzing these interviews was certainly enjoyable, I would not want it to obscure the importance of the learning that resulted from these interviews. I would like to recap what I have learned, what I can share with you and what you as a trader can learn from discussions within these pages.

The Ultimate Capitalist Tool

Of all vehicles that are available to capitalists, the most blatant is without a doubt speculation in stocks and futures. If the goal of a capitalist society is to create more money by using money, the goal of the stock or futures speculator is also to create more money by "less" money. By this I mean that the speculator in stocks may buy stocks on margin, *borrowing* money in the hope of using leverage to produce large percentage gains.

The futures trader is the ultimate capitalist since the margin requirements in most futures markets are often less than ten percent of the total contract value. Naturally, there are two sides to the leverage coin. The negative side is that, in spite of the benefits that leverage can provide, its limitations are considerable.

While the use of margin can facilitate larger gains, it also opens the way to losses that may easily be far greater than the amount invested. Hence, the game of speculation is difficult to win. There are many, many losers and only a relative handful of winners. The leverage vehicle may facilitate large gains or may prompt large losses due to the emotional response it evokes among traders. Emotion is the chief enemy of the speculator unless it is used to his or her advantage.

Emotion is the chief enemy of the speculator unless it is used to his or her advantage.

Although the situation for investors using 50 percent margin in stocks (or even futures) is not nearly as exaggerated as it is for those who speculate in futures using minimal margin, it is similarly difficult for the investor to be consistently successful. Both investors and speculators are victims of human error, poor judgment, emotion and lack of self-confidence.

To achieve consistent results in the ultimate game of capitalism, it is necessary to play the game skillfully and aggressively. However, the game is not readily learned nor willingly taught. Precisely for this reason, those who learn to play the game profitably are respected, honored, rewarded and revered. Even those who are marginally successful are admired because even minimal success is often extremely difficult to achieve.

This is true in virtually any field of endeavor. Those who have achieved great things are respected and studied so that their students may have the opportunity to achieve great results. I hope that by studying the methods that great investors and traders have used in their struggles for success, you will find a way to illuminate your road to profitable investing.

To answer the question at the end of Chapter 1, *why be concerned about these issues?* . . . because they will make success more likely.

Bibliography

Appel, Gerald. *The Five Day Power Thrust Trading System*. Great Neck, NY: Signalert Corporation, 1988.

Appel, Gerald. *The Major Market Bottom Finder*. Great Neck, NY: Signalert Corporation, 1986.

Appel, Gerald. *The Major Trend Power Index*. Great Neck, NY: Signalert Corporation, 1985.

Appel, Gerald. *Selected Readings from Systems and Forecasts*. Great Neck, NY: Signalert Corporation, 1989.

Appel, Gerald. *Stock Market Trading Systems*. Greenville, SC: Traders Press, 1990.

Appel, Gerald. *Time Trend II . . . The Advanced Time Trend Momentum Trading System*. Toronto, CAN: Scientific Investment Systems, Inc., 1982.

Appel, Gerald. *Winning Market Systems—83 Ways To Beat the Market*. Great Neck, NY: Signalert Corporation, 1986.

Babcock, Bruce. *The Business One Irwin Guide to Trading Systems*. Burr Ridge, IL: Irwin Professional Publishing, 1989.

Babcock, Bruce and Peter Brandt. *Trading Commodity Futures with Classical Chart Patterns*. Sacramento, CA: Advanced Trading Seminars, Inc., 1990.

Babcock, Bruce. *Trendiness in the Futures Markets*. Sacramento, CA: CTCR Products, 1993.

Barnes, Robert M. *Taming the Pits: A Technical Approach to Commodity Trading*. New York, NY: Wiley, 1979.

Bernstein, Jacob. *Beyond the Investor's Quotient: The Inner World of Investing*. New York, NY: Wiley, 1988.

Bernstein, Jacob. *Facts on Futures*. Chicago, IL: Probus Publishing, 1987.

Bernstein, Jacob. *The New Investor's Quotient*. New York, NY: Wiley, 1993.

Gold, Gerald. *Modern Commodity Futures Trading*. 7th ed. New York, NY: Commodity Research Bureau, 1975.

Prechter, Robert R., Jr. *Did the Tidal Wave Crest in 1989?* Gainesville, GA: New Classics Library, 1993.

Prechter, Robert R., Jr. and A.J. Frost. *Elliott Wave Principle: Key to Stock Market Profits*. Gainesville, GA: New Classics Library, 1990.

Prechter, Robert R., Jr. *Elliott Wave Theorist Reprints, 1976 to date.* Gainesville, GA: New Classics Library.

Prechter, Robert R., Jr., ed. *The Major Works of R.N. Elliott.* Gainesville, GA: New Classics Library, 1990.

Prechter, Robert R., Jr. *Popular Culture and the Stock Market—A Collection, 1983–1991.* Gainesville, GA: New Classics Library, 1991.

Prechter, Robert R., Jr., ed. *R.N. Elliott's Market Letters, 1938–1946.* Gainesville, GA: New Classics Library, 1993.

Prechter, Robert R., Jr. *Special Reports Collection, 1981 to date.* Gainesville, GA: New Classics Library.

Prechter, Robert R., Jr. *A Turn in the Tidal Wave, Parts I & II.* Gainesville, GA: New Classics Library, 1989.

Wilder, Welles. *The Adam Theory of Markets.* McLeansville, NC: Cavida Ltd., 1987.

Wilder, Welles. *The Delta Phenomenon.* McLeansville, NC: Cavida Ltd., 1991.

Wilder, Welles. *New Concepts in Technical Trading Systems.* McLeansville, NC: Trend Research, 1978.

Wilder, Welles. *The Wisdom of the Ages in Acquiring Wealth.* McLeansville, NC: Cavida Ltd., 1989.

Williams, Larry R. *America's 4 Most Diabolical Legal Strategies.* Solana Beach, CA: CTI Publishing, 1991.

Williams, Larry R. *The Definitive Guide to Futures Trading, Vol. 1.* Brightwaters, NY: Windsor Books, 1988.

Williams, Larry R. *The Definitive Guide to Futures Trading, Vol. 2.* Brightwaters, NY: Windsor Books, 1988.

Williams, Larry R. *How I Made One Million Dollars . . . Last Year . . . Trading Commodities.* Brightwaters, NY: Windsor Books, 1973.

Williams, Larry R. *How Seasonal Factors Influence Commodity Prices.* Brightwaters, NY: Windsor Books, 1977.

Williams, Larry R. *How To Outfox the Foxes.* Solana Beach, CA: CTI Publishing, 1991.

Williams, Larry R. *How To Prosper in the Coming Good Years.* Solana Beach, CA: CTI Publishing, 1982.

Williams, Larry R. *The Mountain of Moses.* Solana Beach, CA: CTI Publishing, 1991.

Williams, Larry R. *19 Amazing Pain Relief Secrets of a Desperate Arthritic.* Solana Beach, CA: CTI Publishing, 1992.

Williams, Larry R. *19 Secrets of a Life Extensionist.* Solana Beach, CA: CTI Publishing, 1992.

Williams, Larry R. and Michelle L. Noseworthy. *Sure Thing Commodity Trading.* Brightwaters, NY: Windsor Books, 1977.

Index